PRAISE FOR
HOW TO LISTEN AND HOW TO BE HEARD

"This must-read book teaches you an approach to handling difficult conversations and offers a roadmap to bring people together for more productive, human connections."

> —DEIRDRE BREAKENRIDGE, author, speaker, and CEO at Pure
> Performance Communications

"If you want to become a more effective communicator, follow Alissa's
valuable advice in *How to Listen and How to Be Heard*. You won't regret
the conversation that happens afterwards."

> —LAURA VANDERKAM, author of *Off the Clock* and *Juliet's
> School of Possibilities*

How to
LISTEN
and How to
BE HEARD

Inclusive Conversations at Work

ALISSA CARPENTER

CAREER
PRESS

This edition first published in 2020 by Career Press, an imprint of
Red Wheel/Weiser, LLC

With offices at:
65 Parker Street, Suite 7
Newburyport, MA 01950
www.careerpress.com
www.redwheelweiser.com

ISBN: 978-1-63265-163-1
Library of Congress Cataloging-in-Publication Data available upon request.

Cover design by Kathryn Sky-Peck
Interior images by Kenny Halsey
Interior by Maureen Forys, Happenstance Type-O-Rama
Typeset in Minion Pro and Auster Rounded with RB No 2.1 and Argyle Socks

Printed in Canada
MAR

10 9 8 7 6 5 4 3 2 1

TO BRIAN, AVERY,
AND XAVIER

CONTENTS

PART IV: Be Comfortable with the Uncomfortable

PART V: The Power of Relationship Building

ACKNOWLEDGMENTS

WRITING A BOOK is never a simple or easy task. In order to get this one into your hands, I had a lot of behind-the-scenes help.

I'd first like to thank John McAdam, who suggested that I write this and helped come up with a rough outline, and Colleen Heavens, who was instrumental in fleshing out those ideas. I'd also like to thank Steve Harris, my literary agent, for believing in this project and bringing it to life.

Many thanks to the subject matter experts who shared their personal stories: Heather Z. Kay, Dr. Scott J. Romeika, Dr. Katherine La Hart, John Herbut, Due Quach, Dr. Janice Asare, Dr. Hoi Ning Ngai, Greg DeShields, Red Coffey, Drew Albert, C. Coffey, Judy M., Celia C., Juan Vasquez, Debbie Roman, Jamie Librot, Taylor D., Karen Swanson, Kristen Topping, Lori Rosenthal, Amy Gallagher, Gary Miciunas, Dr. Amy Cooper Hakim, Christina Merriweather, Rev. Charles Howard PhD, Winne Sun, Jennifer Sherlock, Nicole Stephenson, Brian Coll, Chantel Soumis, Rhona Fromm, Briana Lora, Barbara Taylor, Eleanor Lyons, Darla Still, and the others who wished to remain anonymous.

This book would not have been possible without my parents and in-laws (Mom, Dad, Mark, Hali, Lynne, and Richard) who have always supported me, no matter how out there my ideas have seemed. My brother Mathew also deserves my thanks for his service to our country, for showing me what true resilience and grit look like. My circle of friends and family has also been behind me all the way through this process. They supported me when I took the great leap of opening my own business and have continued to support me as I work my way through the book-writing process.

I also want to thank all the readers for taking the time to read and share this book. This project would not have been possible had it not been for their continued encouragement, social media promotion, referrals, and interest. Thank you for the support and for making an active effort to humanize our workplaces one conversation at a time.

And finally, my kids and husband (Avery, Xavier, and Brian) have been everything to me throughout this process. Their sacrifices and support have meant the world to me. The three of them have inspired my creativity, provided endless supplies of Swedish Fish, and have been my consistent reminder of why I do what I do. I love you.

INTRODUCTION

ACCORDING TO GALLUP'S *State of the American Workplace* report, only 30 percent of employees strongly agree that their opinions count at work.[1] Yes, only 30 percent. So, what does that mean for the other 70 percent? Well, they're likely feeling unheard, unseen, and not understood. Remember the last time someone didn't listen to something you felt was important? When they completely shot down your idea or just ignored it? I'm sure it felt pretty crappy—in all of its "Why am I even in this meeting?" glory.

But why is this the case? What's causing this feeling among so many employees throughout the workplace?

First let's look at how different today's modern workforce really is. Right now, five generations are out there working together, ranging in age from 16 to over 75. And within these generations, more and more diversity has entered the mix. No matter whether you are looking at gender, race, ethnicity, or religion, the workplace doesn't look like it did 50 years ago (or even 10 or 20).

And then mixed in with those differences in age, culture, and whatever else, we have all sorts of different personalities! Who we are and how we think is made up of all of the experiences we've had in our lives up until this point. Each individual brings their own way of seeing things and expressing them into their careers (and around that conference room table). No two people—even if they share similar backgrounds or demographics—have the same perspective.

OK, so after reviewing all of this, it's pretty clear that we have many differences cropping up in the workplace. And it's pretty safe to say that these contribute to why so many employees are having trouble getting through to their colleagues and bosses. So, what do we do about it?

The first step is to recognize that these differences exist, and that they're here to stay. We need to respect and embrace our varied viewpoints, and then we can start to communicate across (not against) them. We need to accept these differences as a natural part of working with others and we need to start *actually* listening to each other. Open your ears to what others have to say. Open your mind to different ideas and ways of thinking. Agree that you're likely to always disagree on some things. But make it a point to at least start talking about what these things are.

This book provides hands-on tools to help you start and guide these important conversations. It covers mediums and phrases to use. Strategies to enact. Physical spaces to build and transform. It explains how taking a novel approach—for something big, or something small—can ultimately create the opportunity for *new* dialogue that gets you moving forward.

We'll talk about how we can break down communication barriers in our modern work environments and how this is just as important in our digital spaces as it is in person (or maybe even more so). We'll cover important questions: How do we connect with our virtual coworkers via technology? How do we navigate change as leaders and as employees? When should we take a conversation out of an email, and into someone's office?

Other chapters talk about how we can make ourselves accessible to build relationships; why it's important to be transparent and always put all of our cards on the table; and how to say no while still fostering a culture of openness and creativity. We'll get into tackling challenges like departmental divides, the silo effect, and toxic coworkers.

And we'll also talk about some crucial—and sometimes hard-to-have—discussions that need to start happening. How do we openly talk about diversity, inclusion, and belonging? How do we get out of our comfort zones and start genuinely trying to understand where people are coming from? How do we make our workplaces more . . . human?

Ultimately, I hope you use the tools in this book to develop stronger teams that are built on trust and authentic communication. This doesn't mean everyone will be best friends or high-fiving across cubicles. But it will mean respect, clarity, and directness—all made possible with more productive communication.

The majority of the advice in this book applies to both managers and non-managers and can be used by employees at all levels of an organization. If you are a manager, use your influence to implement these strategies and make your teams better. If you're not a manager and read about an idea that would make sense in your organization, bring it up to your supervisor. Let's not think in terms of us versus them. We're all in this together.

Remember, though, there are no quick fixes. Working toward change takes time. It takes conscious effort. This book is a good start for getting everyone on the same page, or at least in the same room, but I would be doing you a disservice if I said it answers any and all questions about working in diverse workplaces. People and environments are constantly changing and evolving, and each individual coworker or supervisor is always a person all their own. You should mold and adapt the strategies you find in the pages that follow, including the "Human Connections" I've included from other content experts, to your own particular situations and relationships.

But also remember this: Every employee within an organization can provide value. Every. Single. One. Everyone is in a position of power to bring change to their role, to their unit, and to the overall success of an organization. What makes you different is what makes you great. So, learn to appreciate these differences in your colleagues, and understand how these things might impact how they think, act, or feel in the workplace. Doing so might be hard or uncomfortable, but invest in getting there. One conversation at a time.

To continue learning, head to *www.notokthatsokcoach.com/book* for additional resources and videos.

PART I

The Advantages of Our Differences

CHAPTER 1

Putting Our
Strengths into Action

THE BEST EMPLOYEES bring something to the table that no one else can. But sometimes these talents and strengths are overlooked, underutilized, or even mistaken for weaknesses. When we don't know each other's strengths, we're not maximizing the effectiveness of the conversations we can have, and we're not making efficient use of our talent resources. Taking the time to uncover each of our strengths helps us understand why people communicate in certain ways and what information they need to make decisions. Doing so also provides us with insight into how we can adjust our own communication styles to be more effective, and it helps us get to the bottom of why we seem to butt heads with certain people, while having better synergy with others.

While at work, have you ever encountered these scenarios?

- Have you been a part of a brainstorm session where a few people seem to have all the ideas while others silently listen?

- Have you had a supervisor who constantly looks for more data and facts before making a decision on beginning a new project, while you have been ready to start the project since before you even talked to your supervisor?

- Have you had a colleague who stops meetings and goes around the room to see if anyone else has anything to say, which adds another 20 minutes to your already long meeting?

- Have you had a peer who's always 10 steps ahead of everyone else while thinking through a project, while you're just trying to focus on what needs to be done by the end of the day?

These are just a few examples of diverse strengths being applied in the workplace. We all think and act differently, and although certain actions may be frustrating to you, they are not necessarily bad. This is how others utilize their strengths to benefit their work, and they should not be thought of as right or wrong. In fact, the way you conduct yourself in meetings at work may be just as frustrating to others. If you don't know where someone is coming from, or why they complete tasks the way they do, it can be infuriating.

For instance, the people who are silent in your brainstorm session might be deliberating about what to say and how to say it. They might not talk a lot, but when they do, it is logical, well thought out, and can be something no one else has thought of before.

And that supervisor who always wants data to support their decisions? It might appear to you as if they're holding you back from moving forward, but they're likely working through potential pitfalls and managing risk for the success of the project. They're concerned about doing things right (and thoroughly) the first time.

The annoying colleague who spends extra time going around the room to get feedback is making sure everyone's opinion is heard. Doing so might make the meeting go longer (eye rolls inserted here), but what they really want is to ensure that the group is not missing any details and that all attendees feel valued and are given the chance to share their insight.

And your peer who is already 10 steps ahead? What they're really doing is thinking about the future and what the project will look like as a whole. It's important to them to be inspired by thinking about what could be and how what you're working on right now will positively impact the big picture.

HUMAN CONNECTION

I was working with a team to put together a self- and management assessment. There was an employee from IT, a project manager, and two representatives from human resources (including myself) on our team. I wanted to ensure that people's strengths were coming out and that I was using them correctly. We all had previously taken the CliftonStrengths assessment to identify our top five talents.

During the process, the project manager was always looking for background information. She would ask questions about what had been done in the past that led us to this point to make a change. She wanted to understand the history so she could make better decisions moving forward. She was utilizing her strength of Context.

My colleague in human resources wanted deadlines and deliverables throughout the process to ensure he knew what he was responsible for and to keep others on track, which was his strength of Responsibility. The IT staff member used his Futuristic strength and asked a lot of questions to get a better understanding of the project. He wanted to look past the utilization of the tool to see how we would implement the assessment in our performance conversations. He also wanted to know what reports would need to be generated and how leaders and managers would be using that data. These pertinent questions helped him design the form in a way that would allow us to filter reports to meet our needs.

This project was really interesting because we were all attacking the same problem, but from different perspectives. Once we understood each other's strengths and why we were either asking questions, wanting deadlines, or needing context, it made it easier for us to work together. We achieved a better result because we knew where we were all coming from.

HEATHER Z. KAY, Gallup Certified Strengths Coach

Identifying Strengths

When we inspect the preceding scenarios with this lens, we can see how our employees, coworkers, and supervisors used their strengths to enhance the team. But when we're living through such instances, it feels like the people we work with are going out of their way to make our job harder. In reality, they're applying their strengths to work through things in their own way.

A *strength* is something that comes naturally to us and gives us the highest confidence in the outcome we produce. We all have strengths. Even if you don't realize it, you are subconsciously acting in certain ways because of them. And although it's great that we all have them, how can we proactively identify them for ourselves and others? How can identifying these strengths give us perspective on how we apply them? Likewise, how can we use them to better understand our colleagues? Here are some suggestions:

Look inward. It can be hard to look internally, identify what makes you unique, and see what you bring to the table. Move beyond the basic, "What are my strengths?" and ask yourself specific questions:

- What do my coworkers rely on me most for?
- During which tasks do I lose track of time?
- What am I working on right now that I'm excited about?
- What is an accomplishment I'm proud of and why?

Ask directly. When you're trying to identify your teammates' or employees' strengths, reframe the questions above and ask them directly:

- "What do your coworkers rely on you most for?"
- "During which tasks do you lose track of time?"
- "What are you working on right now that you're excited about?"
- "What is an accomplishment you're proud of and why?"

Ask others. Another way to gain perspective on your coworkers' strengths is to ask people who work with them on a consistent and ongoing basis. It can be the colleague that sits next to them or an employee in another department who uses them as a resource.

- "What type of work do they tend to ask to do?"
- "What energizes them?"
- "What tasks make them light up?"
- "When do they seem most engaged?"

Observe. Take time to observe others' strengths in action. It's not necessarily about what they're doing, but how they're doing it. Two people can accomplish the same task, but they might go about it in different ways. Whereas one person might gather data to make a decision, another may speak to colleagues and gather previous experiences. Look at how they're successfully accomplishing their tasks. Don't turn this into a National Geographic research assignment, but do it casually to observe your coworkers acting naturally.

Take an assessment, psychometric assessment, or inventory. Several assessments help us identify how and why we work the way we do. Some of the more popular ones are CliftonStrengths (Gallup), Everything DiSC (Wiley), and Character Strengths (The VIA Institute on Character).[1] By bringing these inventories and assessments to your organization, you have made it possible for everyone to have a common language and to more easily understand each other's strengths.

ASSESSMENT, PSYCHOMETRIC ASSESSMENT, OR INVENTORY	DESCRIPTION
CliftonStrengths	▪ Measures the greatest potential for building strength by identifying recurring patterns of thought, feeling, and behavior.
	▪ The positive psychology approach focuses on 34 talent themes within four domains of leadership (Relationship Building, Influencing, Strategic Thinking, Executing).[2]

ASSESSMENT, PSYCHOMETRIC ASSESSMENT, OR INVENTORY	DESCRIPTION
Everything DiSC	■ Measures the degree of Dominance, Influence, Steadiness, and Conscientious behavior. ■ Focuses on how someone prefers to act, what they do, and their behavior.[3]
VIA Character Strengths	■ Measures positive traits of personality present not only during times of excellence but in everyday moments and in times of resilience. ■ The positive psychology approach focuses on 24 VIA character strengths that are the pathways to each of the five areas of well-being (positive emotion, more engagement, better relationships, more meaning, more accomplishments).[4]

When we're able to identify people using their strengths and begin appreciating them, real change can happen. We'll then start to see employees looking forward to going to work, having more positive interactions with others, and coming up with innovative solutions to complex tasks.

TACTICS TO IDENTIFY STRENGTHS

✔ Look inward.

✔ Ask directly.

✔ Observe.

✔ Take an assessment, psychometric assessment, or inventory.

Cluing into Strengths

Through these conversations, you'll most likely uncover things that you never knew about yourself, colleagues, supervisors, and employees. It's pretty rare that we take the opportunity to step back and reflect on what we enjoy doing and what comes naturally to us in the workplace. This makes it even more important to listen attentively for cues and clues that can help us make the most out of our strengths.

In my work with clients, I use CliftonStrengths to identify individual talents to create more cohesive teams. Within the context of this assessment, the talent themes fall into four domains.[5]

Relationship Building	Influencing
Accept and include others, bring people together, actively listen	Help others get their voices heard, be able to sell ideas, and convince others
Strategic Thinking	**Executing**
Analyze information to inform their decisions by thinking about current and future problems	Set goals and have the stamina to get things done quickly and accurately

Whether or not you use the CliftonStrengths/Gallup assessment, these four domains provide a good framework of the talents to look for. When you're creating teams, not only is it important to have people who are creative and come up with great ideas but also to have individuals who can sell those ideas to others. In addition, you want people who can spot pitfalls and have strategic back-up plans, along with employees who help others get their voices heard and know who to bring together in the first place.

In your conversations and self-reflection, listen for people who

- Put plans into action
- Ask targeted and strategic questions
- Others want to be around
- Can sell snow to a snowman
- Bring diverse groups of people together

These strengths can show themselves in a variety of ways:

- Maybe Donna is always making lists and checking things off. This could be a sign of her strength to keep track of tasks and follow through. She may be the person you rely on to make sure the team finishes what they started and who knows what they're supposed to be doing in the first place.

- Maybe Linda is always taking the time to coach younger staff and teach them the ropes. This could be a sign of her strength in development. She would be a great asset when you're bringing in new hires and may be able to lead employee orientation.

- Maybe Yale is always organizing group happy hours and showing his strength for bringing people together. His energetic spirit is just what the group needs when you're having a tough quarter.

- Maybe Natalie is always stopping at people's desks to strike up a conversation. Her strength of communicating with others is an asset and can be leveraged during prospective client meetings and networking events.

These subtle (and not so subtle) actions are important to look out for, especially if you notice a pattern. Take note of them and use this information to inform future conversations, team development, and task assignments.

Individual Strengths Equal Stronger Teams

Now that you have a better grasp on your teammates' strengths, it's time to engage in authentic communication. Through these conversations, you can gain a better perspective on the way they work, while sharing your appreciation of what they bring to the team. This also gives you the chance to be more strategic about what projects you assign or ask for in hopes of producing more efficient and creative outcomes. To get the most out of your coworkers', your employees', and your own personal strengths, try these strategies:

Provide strengths-based feedback. Share exactly how you saw your employee's strengths in action. How did they enhance the team, project, assignment, or organization as a whole? What unique contribution did they make? "Xavier, I was impressed with how you were able to get our team to openly share their ideas at the last meeting. Your individualized approach helped us gather some great concepts for the project."

As a peer, take a moment to compliment your coworker. "Myla, I was really impressed with the presentation you gave to the investors yesterday. You were really confident, answered their questions with ease, and I learned a lot about our new initiatives. Thank you for volunteering to do it."

Align tasks with strengths. Move past a one-size-fits-all management style and tailor projects to the strengths of individual employees. Make an effort to be more proactive in what responsibilities you assign by asking what your employees enjoy working on and what they want to learn. Employees who do work they enjoy and are good at are more engaged and more likely to see a future with their company.

As an employee, reflect on the projects you're currently working on and ask your supervisor for other work that aligns with your strengths. "I really enjoy speaking on behalf of our group to the investors. Are there any upcoming opportunities to do that?"

Find unique professional development opportunities. Whether it is by providing occasions for employees to take a course, attend a conference, or speak at a seminar, explore ways for your employees to build on their strengths. If you're sent an email invitation for a professional development event, invite an employee to join you, or pass the invitation along to an employee or colleague who you think would like it.

As an employee, make it a point to advocate for yourself and ask to register for an online course or program that aligns with your strengths. Specifically share how this will benefit the organization. "Brian, I would like to go to the annual sales conference in May. The agenda is packed with sessions that focus on building relationships as part of the sales process. This is a strength of mine that I would like to take to the next level to land Games Inc. as our new client."

HUMAN CONNECTION

It's easy to stay in the bubble of the day-to-day in the workplace, but professional development can really enhance an employee's growth and long-term retention. As an organization, we recognize its importance and give each staff member the opportunity to attend at least one event, if not more. During my quarterly review meetings, I make an active effort to bring up opportunities and gauge interest in specific areas. This helps me to be more targeted in making suggestions for upcoming events, certifications, and courses. I actively forward emails and flyers, and have one-on-one conversations on opportunities aligned with their interests. I want my employees to know that I am invested in their professional success and will advocate for additional resources and development on their behalf.

SCOTT J. ROMEIKA, Senior Director of Academic and Student Affairs of the Wharton School of the University of Pennsylvania

Form diverse teams. Bring together employees with various strengths. Find people who are creative and strategic thinkers, who follow through, and who influence others to make decisions. When we create teams of people who all think and act similarly, we're missing out on new concepts and the ability to challenge ideas to come up with better solutions.

Ask the peers you asked to join the team for their input or critical feedback on what you're working on. Did you miss anything? Is there something they would adjust or change? Identify peers who look at things differently. This will bring your assignment to the next level.

Focus on the result. As a manager or team leader, when you focus more on the *what,* like deadlines and expectations, as opposed to giving specific direction on the *how* to get it done, you're letting employees play to their strengths to figure it out. Share the results you're looking for without micromanaging the details of how employees need to go about a specific project, while still making sure they're following the internal controls in completing the project. For example, if your nonprofit has a group goal of $100,000 for this campaign, and individual goals of $10,000 per team member, let each member of your team share how they plan to raise the money. One person may volunteer to teach a series of workout classes in exchange for donations, while another might meet one on one with their donor connections.

Be vulnerable. Let your colleagues know when they get the best of you, the worst of you, what they can count on you for, and what you need from them to do your job. "I need time to research before coming up with new concepts." "You get the best version of me when you provide me with the space to think through ideas." "You can count on me to spot pitfalls and come up with alternative solutions." "You get the worst side of me when I feel rushed or put on the spot to provide information or be creative."

Get an outsider's perspective. Consider bringing in a consultant or outside company to assess the strengths of your teams and employees to maximize their abilities. It can be hard to participate in trainings if you're the one leading them, so getting someone with a fresh perspective (from outside your workplace dynamics) can take your team to the next level.

STRATEGIES TO TAP INTO STRENGTHS

✔ Provide strengths-based feedback.

✔ Align tasks with strengths.

✔ Find unique professional development opportunities.

✔ Form diverse teams.

✔ Focus on the result.

✔ Be vulnerable.

✔ Get an outsider's perspective.

BE HUMAN. ACT HUMAN.

Although our strengths can be a huge asset in the workplace, they can also cause a lot of drama. When we don't understand why people work the way they do, it's easy to get frustrated and not appreciate their contributions, especially when we would go about it a different way. But understanding and leveraging our strengths—and the strengths of those who work with and for us—leads to enhanced productivity and engagement.

CHAPTER 2

Navigating the Multigenerational Workforce

WHEN WE TALK about generations, we're not just talking about a standard set of birth years. Generations are defined by technology, pivotal events, sociological trends, and economics during our formative years. These areas shape the way we think about the world around us and guide our interactions with others.

But what happens when we work with people from other generations and don't understand where they're coming from? What do we do when someone is stuck in their own generational work style?

- We start perpetuating stereotypes about a generation.
- We link differences to lack of competence and work ethic.
- We avoid others because we don't know the best medium in which to communicate.
- We provide old incentives that no longer motivate or inspire.
- We don't achieve personal or professional growth because we're stuck in our ways.

Even in what seem to be the best workplace environments, communication breakdowns are bound to happen with varying personalities and age groups. If we don't try to understand the situations and experiences that make us who we are, we'll be stuck in a breakdown loop. The first step to moving forward is to have conversations across generations and get to know the people we work with.

One of the exercises I do when facilitating workplace trainings is to have participants create a timeline of major national events that happened during their childhood. Examples of these include 9/11, the 2008 recession, the Great Depression, legalization of gay marriage, the rise of social media and computers, and civil rights activism. Each participant then shares how this event has impacted their life, their communication preference and style, and their interactions with others. Answers vary from having less trust in large systems like banks to being able to see daily pictures of their grandchildren on Facebook.

This icebreaker helps provide some insight into how these shared experiences affected our lives, even if we may not have realized it. It's a starting-off point for future discussions on deeper issues that can influence the way we work together.

Although it's important to have these conversations and navigate multigenerational workforces to understand why we act the way we do, we should not box in or generalize all people within a generation. Generations are made of individuals, not carbon copies or robots. However, understanding and navigating this landscape will help us identify ways to communicate and motivate *individuals* within the generations.

Five Generations in the Workforce

Currently five generations are in the workforce (Traditionalists/Silent Generation, Baby Boomers, Gen X, Millennials, and Gen Z). In general, each one is looking for something different from their coworkers, supervisors, and organizations. Understanding these differences can help us tap into more meaningful conversations that will help retain employees in the long term and keep our relationships strong. Let's look at each generation and how to tap into their key motivators. Remember, this doesn't apply to every person in each generation, but it does give you a better idea of where they might be coming from.

Traditionalists

Traditionalists were born between 1925 and 1946. Many were raised during the Great Depression and value their jobs. Many have also worked for one company over the lifetime of their career, are extremely loyal, and get along well with their colleagues.

In the workplace, a Traditionalist might be known as the figure-head of an organization. This rings true especially with family-owned businesses that have been passed down to future generations. Although many Traditionalists are retired, some are also being asked to come back on a consulting basis to help the newer generations navigate the business. The key to working with Traditionalists is to keep them up to speed on the technology used within the organization and to create environments in which they feel valued and not pushed aside for a newer model.

Top motivators. Respect and recognition. Give subtle and personalized recognition and feedback. Take the time to say thank you and acknowledge their service to the organization. Talk about their positive impact on getting newer employees up to speed. It's important to respect how they've accomplished tasks in the past, while working together to find new solutions.

What they bring to the table. Traditionalists bring institutional knowledge and a strong work ethic.

Baby Boomers

Baby Boomers were born between 1946 and 1964. Although, on average, about 10,000 Boomers are retiring each day, many are choosing to stay in the workforce either full- or part-time.[1] Because the 2008 recession forced many to deplete their retirement funds and modern medicine is helping them live longer and healthier lives, this generation is extending their stay in the workforce. Baby Boomers are known for their optimism and their value of hard work.

Compared to the previous generation, Boomers grew up being surrounded by more people in their families, neighborhoods, and classrooms. This helped them develop a sense of comradery and com-petition.[2] Although Boomers may not have grown up with computers, it's important to not underestimate their interest and knowledge in the newest technology. They have been building in-person relationships for as long as they can remember, so if there is a barrier between them and the person they are trying to interact with, it can be a turn-off. Boomers also have a lot of crucial institutional knowledge to pass along, and if we don't tap into it, it will go out the door with them when they retire.

Top motivators. Acknowledgment and financial stability. Take time to recognize their efforts and service to the organization in person and with financial compensation. Look for opportunities for them to mentor employees and for them to be seen as valued experts. As they're retiring, they're continuing to plan for financial stability beyond their time within your organization, so financial recognition through bonuses and other means are coveted.

What they bring to the table. Boomers are optimistic and hardworking.

Gen X

Gen Xers were born between 1965 and 1980. This generation is also known for being *latchkey kids* as they usually came home from school to an empty home, the first generation with both parents in the workforce. In many cases, they were responsible for themselves and their siblings. So, as independent children, they grew into independent employees who get the job done and desire to work without micromanagement.

As managers, Gen Xers also expect others to work independently with little direction. They want to make an impact and be proud of what they accomplish at work. They can often find it difficult to be passed up for promotions in favor of younger generations. Many have waited a long time for their Baby Boomer bosses to retire and feel overlooked in favor of Millennials who swooped in for a role the Gen Xers sought. They want to work on meaningful projects where they can tap into their years of knowledge and experience.

Top motivators. Autonomy and work/life balance. Give them an assignment and let them run with it without constantly checking in on their progress. Explore alternative ways for them to work from home and other locations.

What they bring to the table. Gen Xers are self-starters, responsible, and results driven.

Millennials

Millennials were born between 1980 and 1996. Millennials grew up with rapidly improving technology, from pagers to smart phones. When they were children, they typically had jam-packed schedules filled with after-school activities. They are used to working with teams, receiving participation trophies, and eating avocado toast (OK, not all of them), and they value mentoring and coaching from their supervisors. Millennials see advancement as something that is earned through their outcomes—like what they produce or achieve—and not through tenure or time spent in the office.

Millennials are helpers looking to make their mark and quickly move up in the workforce while advocating for work/life balance. They like to make processes more efficient and don't understand having to stick around the office if they've completed their work for the day. They are quick to move on to another opportunity if one presents itself or if they aren't moving quickly enough in their current role. This can lead to employers being frustrated about their level of loyalty.

Top motivators. Access, opportunity to learn and grow, and work/life balance. Provide consistent and ongoing feedback and access to higher-level meetings where they can share their ideas. Give them an opportunity to flex their muscles and learn something new, and embrace their desire for collaboration.

What they bring to the table. Millennials are confident, globally minded, and purpose-driven.

Gen Z

Gen Z was born between 1996 and 2010. Technology has always been a part of their lives; they don't remember a time without social media or the internet, and most were never exposed to the peril of dial-up internet. Although they like to work in groups, they want to know how their individual contribution had an impact on the team as well as how their team did. Gen Z wants space to think outside the box, freedom to identify a new process or procedure, and the flexibility to work on their side hustle or passion project.

Top motivators. Community involvement, opportunities for flexible learning, work/life balance. Take them seriously, listen to their ideas, give public praise, and provide opportunities for them to learn through technology. Make them part of creating sustainable change and finding ways to give back to the community. Provide social rewards for completion of learning programs and initiate reverse mentoring opportunities.

What they bring to the table. Gen Z is tech savvy, values diversity, and is socially responsible.

You might be thinking: Why isn't money the first thing on each of these lists of motivators? Don't get me wrong, everyone wants to be compensated fairly. But just throwing around money without more thoughtful strategies isn't going to work with the new generations of employees. They want to be part of work cultures that provide more than just a steady paycheck. They want to know they're making a difference and consistently learning new skills while working with people they enjoy being around.

GENERATION	TOP MOTIVATORS	WHAT THEY BRING
Traditionalists	▪ Respect	▪ Institutional knowledge
	▪ Recognition	▪ Strong work ethic
Baby Boomers	▪ Acknowledgment	▪ Optimistic
	▪ Financial stability	▪ Hard working

GENERATION	TOP MOTIVATORS	WHAT THEY BRING
Gen Xers	▪ Autonomy ▪ Work/life balance	▪ Self-starters ▪ Responsible ▪ Results driven
Millennials	▪ Access ▪ Opportunity to learn and grow ▪ Work/life balance	▪ Confident ▪ Globally minded ▪ Purpose driven
Gen Zers	▪ Community involvement ▪ Opportunities for flexible learning ▪ Work/life balance	▪ Tech savvy ▪ Value diversity ▪ Socially responsible

Stop Generation Shaming

Regardless of their generation, everyone wants to be valued, respected, and heard. But each one of us might express our thoughts and receive information differently. One of my clients was struggling with how some of their Baby Boomer employees were trying to build personal relationships with Millennial employees. A few of these employees read articles that recommended specific methods for communicating with each generation. The Boomer employees then went on to use this information to inform how they communicated with all of their coworkers of various generations. They walked to the offices of their Baby Boomer peers, emailed Gen X colleagues, and texted Millennials. On the surface, this seemed fine, but it soon started to stir up some controversy because people did not understand why they were getting an email, when someone else was getting a face-to-face conversation. By limiting in-person conversation to only certain coworkers, these employees unintentionally made others feel left out and undervalued.

A Millennial client I spoke with had just started with a new company and was used to instant messaging (IMing) members of their team and supervisor to ask questions. At their old company, this was an established protocol and an easier way for coworkers to communicate with one another without leaving their spaces. A few weeks into their new role, many Baby Boomers on their team voiced frustration at the constant pinging through IM, which was interrupting their workflow; in addition, they were having a hard time keeping up with the pace of the typed conversation. The more seasoned employees were used to popping into one another's offices and sending emails to ask questions and gain clarification. The new employee's primary form of communication was seen as more of a distraction than an efficient communication method.

A Gen X client of mine had a question for a Millennial employee and opted to give them a call on their cell phone. The Millennial answered the phone and was not only frustrated that their coworker had called, but that they hadn't texted first to see if it was OK. The Millennial employee saw it as an invasion of privacy and wanted a text to give them a heads up.

What's the missing component in these scenarios? An initial conversation. Although the chart below provides general tips for communication preferences, it's essential to ask individuals one of these variations:

- "What is the best way to communicate with you?"

- "What is your preferred method of communication?"

- "How can I best get in touch with you if I have a question?"

Maybe your Millennial peer would rather you pop into their office and your Baby Boomer colleague wants a text. You'll never know unless you ask. And it will give you a better idea as to why you have 10 missed calls and no voicemails. Remember, generations are made up of individual people—not clones!

GENERATION	COMMUNICATION PREFERENCE
Traditionalist	**Direct, in-person conversation:** Share information and facts first, followed by exactly what you want them to complete including a timeline. **Handwritten:** Although you might not be writing agendas or notes with paper and pen, be prepared to receive and accept information in this form unless you explicitly state that you need it electronically.

GENERATION	COMMUNICATION PREFERENCE
Baby Boomer	■ **Structure:** Provide a well-written agenda before meetings and outlined structure for projects and assignments. ■ **Scheduled conversation:** Set aside time for formal and scheduled in-person communication. ■ **Informative emails:** Send educational emails that provide value.
Gen X	■ **Informal conversations:** Pop in to their workspace to ask a question and have an impromptu versus all-scheduled meeting. ■ **Email:** Use email to communicate. This allows them to work on their own time schedule and share information. ■ **Brief overview:** They want basic questions answered: What is the task and when is it due? What do I need to do to get it done? Once these questions are answered, they want to complete the assignment with little oversight.
Millennial	■ **Structure and clear goals:** Give them clear deadlines and expectations for assignments and projects. ■ **Instant communication:** Send quick texts or messages instead of long emails. ■ **Reciprocal dialogue:** Include them in the conversation and don't dictate how they need to do something; focus on the results you're looking for.
Gen Z	■ **Instant communication:** Find time to provide frequent, quick, and preferably daily feedback. This can be in person or through technology and can take less than five minutes, no lengthy emails are needed. ■ **Infotainment:** Share information in quick and fun ways, short videos reviewing a process and on-demand learning for new skills. ■ **Structure, clear directions, and transparency:** Be specific about what you would like them to accomplish and share any updates/insights; don't hide information or resources.

Interestingly, one of the most effective ways to communicate across generations is face to face. Despite being brought up with technology, even the younger generations are looking for more in-person contact. According to a study conducted by Randstad and Future Workplace,

53 percent of Gen Z and Millennials prefer in-person communication over tools like instant messaging and video conferencing. In fact, fewer than 20 percent of both generations prefer email.[3] This is something to keep in mind as emails seemingly dominate our communications. Millennials and Gen Z rank it as one of their less preferred communication methods and would rather talk with you face to face.

Communication Partnerships

Reverse mentoring is a great way to give employees of two different generations (typically one older and one younger) a chance to learn from one another. It's a mutual partnership that helps bridge skill gaps and can be a refreshing change of pace for both parties. For example, a Gen Z employee may be able to share their experience working with the latest social sharing website with the Boomer and explain how using it can increase sales of a new product, whereas the Boomer may be able to provide the Gen Z employee with access to higher-level meetings. This access can give the Gen Z employee a chance to meet the senior leadership team. Unlike your typical mentor/mentee relationship, both parties are teaching and learning from each other. Some opportunities for discussion include sharing the following:

- Emerging trends, technology, and products within your industry
- Institutional knowledge of policies and procedures
- Strategies to enhance interpersonal relationships and soft skills
- Untapped outlets to reach a younger demographic
- Preferred mediums to better communicate with your staff

The Ageless Challenge of Communication

No matter what you know about someone else and their generation, there is always the potential for communication hiccups. And ultimately, these issues can get in the way of you making progress with your coworkers and supervisors. Regardless of the medium you use to deliver your message, the barriers discussed next will quickly halt your conversations—or prevent them from even happening in the first place.

The Balancing Act

Even if you uncover the preferred method of communication, it can seem like you're doing a lot of juggling. Hali would rather you pop in his office, Rachel wants a text, Howard only wants to talk on the phone, and Jeff loves sending everything through IM. As you're trying to piece together everyone's preferences, you might find yourself wondering why you asked in the first place.

The key to juggling preferences is to find a place of mutual understanding. If you don't, you'll find yourself covering your office with sticky notes, sending yourself reminders of everyone's personal favorites, or just choosing what you prefer. During your initial communication conversations, nail down how you can contact one another for questions that need immediate answers and action. "If one of my clients needs a work order processed by the end of the business day, what is the best way to reach you?" During these cases, you usually want to defer to their communication preference to ensure that you get the answers you need in time.

For nonurgent matters, work together on a plan in which you're both leaning in and provide the "why" behind it so you're both on the same page. For instance: "I appreciate that you would prefer to have a text conversation when you have questions about client documentation. Although I understand that this method may be easier, this information is confidential and needs to be recorded in our system and tracked for billing purposes. I would be happy to give you a heads up via text that I sent an email if that would help."

If you're having a conversation with your manager, consider leaning in more to their preferred communication style. At the end of the day, if you want a response, it's about the receiver's preference and not the sender's.

"Don't Patronize Me, Sweetie"

Although your coworkers or managers may be the same age as your parents, grandparents, children, or even grandchildren, they should not be treated as if they are. When you treat someone like your flaky little sister or talk to someone like they're your grandmother who cannot figure out how to unlock her phone—you're talking down to them. Phrases like "Well, dear, that's not how we do it around here," "You're so cute, just like my grandma," or "Aw, that's so sweet that you think it will work" all fall under this umbrella. Just because someone is older, doesn't mean they don't understand technology. And just because someone is younger, doesn't make their suggestion any less important to listen to.

HUMAN CONNECTION

When I was working in retail full time, my manager was more than 10 years younger than me. She was a remarkable young woman who had been in the industry since she was 16. She knew her job and performed it very well. She was very business minded and was able to communicate the value of every employee, making her easy to respect and appreciate. I learned a great deal from her.

It was a fairly common occurrence that customers would come into the store and want to speak to the manager and then stand in front of me. The assumption was that because I was senior in age, I was of course the senior in position. I would just smile and call for my young boss and explain that she was the manager and I was still in training! Most people apologized and laughed. On occasion one would argue, thinking I was just trying to blow them off.

As I continued in retail, I found myself in a place where I was hiring staff who were the same age as and some even younger than my children. The challenge here was to stay professional, to manage the staff member and not parent the child.

JUDY, Former Retail Professional

"My Boss Is How Old?"

When we don't trust people, it's hard to have an authentic conversation. This is especially true when younger employees are supervising others of an older generation. These young supervisors and leaders are often questioned about whether they know what they're doing and why they got the job over someone with more tenure at the organization.

If you're a younger manager, be honest with your employees and ask them for support and to share their experiences. "I recognize that I am newer in this role and many of you have been with the company for several years. I value your knowledge and experience and am looking forward to working with and learning from you."

This can be an awkward situation, and it may be even a little embarrassing for older employees who are now answering to a younger manager. But you need to build trust with your team through honesty, action, and consistent transparency. Communicate to them that you need their knowledge and support in order for your team to be successful. For instance, you might say, "Betty, I know you have a ton of experience working with this client. Do you think we could meet sometime this week to share your pointers with me?"

HUMAN CONNECTION

There have been numerous occasions where I have been younger than other employees on my team. I've heard them say that I wasn't deserving to be in my role because "I haven't done my time" like they have. And why would the company hire someone "so young and inexperienced?" On one occasion, I decided to speak up about the hurtful comments of one coworker and said, "Time is only what you make of it and I work hard to make every minute count. However, if you think I'd benefit from your experience and you are willing to share your knowledge to better support the team, I'd love to have the opportunity to learn from you, and I'd appreciate you sharing your candid thoughts."

One of my peers overheard our conversation, and said to my coworker, "You could also benefit from taking some reverse mentoring from this young mind, and if you did, you'd know that she has no need to prove herself, because she will outperform every individual on this team, and she'll be the best team player and genuine person you have ever worked with." After our very public conversation, I asked the individual who made the hurtful comment one on one if they would be my mentor and educate me on the experiences that they thought I could learn from. They also asked for my mentorship. We formed a personal and professional relationship and, over time, they admitted that it was nice seeing a different and new perspective and understood why I was hired. They also apologized for their previous comments.

I learned that you should always try to keep an open mind and give your team members the benefit of the doubt, even if they may not have that same mindset. We can all benefit from helping and learning from one another. It's such a simple practice, but one that is not practiced enough.

KATHERINE LA HART, PhD of Business Administration

"I Don't Need Any Help"

No one wants to be the one who doesn't know how to do something. Especially if that person has been at the company for a long time and is used to people coming to them for answers. It can be difficult for older generations to ask younger colleagues for support on a project or about how to use a newer piece of technology. If you notice someone struggling, ask if you can lend a hand. "What do you need from me to be more comfortable with our new learning management system?" If you're the one struggling and are looking for support, find a colleague with whom you've developed a relationship and start there. They may not know the answer, but they might be able to point you in the direction of someone who does. For example, "Arthur, would you be able to show me how our new phone system works? I'm having a hard time transferring calls."

It's a lot easier to ask for help from people you have a relationship with than to ask someone you hardly know.

"I Know It All"

When employees have an idea that they're excited and passionate about, they tend to share it and try to get everyone on board. It's commonly shared that Millennials tend to be quick to provide a solution or suggestion and don't always approach the situation in a tactful way. You could be in the middle of explaining something and someone else jumps in, pushing their newer and better way. Or worse, someone is not open to learning new information because they think they know it all. Have conversations as a group on when and how to present new ideas. You don't want to belittle anyone's concept or stifle any creativity, but it's important to address how these things should be presented. It's also important to keep an open mind and know that you can learn something from any conversation.

HUMAN CONNECTION

The ink from my diploma had barely dried and I was in a conference room with my boss, an innovative and out-of-the-box thinker, and directors of IT, Marketing, Compliance, Operations, and Legal. They had all been with the business for many years and knew the ins and outs of the industry. They were asking me, the recent college graduate, how I thought we could reengage the business of nearly one thousand employees. I saw it as a test: they wanted to see if I was going to use the opportunity to get on my soapbox or if I was going to make real use of the time. I had ideas (what I now know were naïve aspirations and ideals), but I hadn't established my credibility, and this was my moment—I was either going to blow them away with an idea that they never heard before or reframe the situation. I wasn't confident enough (or knowledgeable enough) to spit out some revolutionary idea for employee engagement (and let's face it, these professionals would most likely have seen, heard, and probably tried whatever I was going to suggest), so before I shared my idea I asked, "Well what has been done before? What did employees experience before and what did they like; what would they never want to do?"

Conversation ensued and I learned that the business had a very risk-averse approach—the teams were forged together with seniority and relationships—and that the average age of employees was close to forty (a stark contrast from my days of working with early-twenty-something year olds). This key finding showed that by me asking questions and not just listening, but actively listening, I was building trust. I showed respect for the leaders by gathering information before blurting out the sexy new organizational topic I just read about in *Harvard Business Review*. I wanted to gamify the workplace, and before I could say that, I had to work with my boss and those very leaders to make sure this idea would actually take root in the office. I had to make sure it wasn't just my idea but *our* idea.

After discussing the past practices of the business, I suggested this generic answer: "Let's make it fun! After all, engagement is about having fun and being invested in something you're interested in." And then the meeting ended. I walked back to my office with my boss. When we got there, he challenged me: "What is fun?" I didn't know, but neither did he, nor did anyone else in the meeting, and that's where the team came in: we needed to work together to establish fun. My boss and I worked diligently over the next few months researching experiential learning and recruiting consultants to design simple, yet effective, games. Months later, we had developed the "Strategy Engagement Path," where we went from team to team and spoke about the business, the strategy, challenges in the industry, and how each department contributed to the overall mission. There were your standard business presentations and periods of competition to link each team's work back to the bigger mission of the company. At the end of the path, the teams would map themselves on our strategy map and explain how they affected the overall business (and of course we had an award ceremony to crown the victors, and these weren't Millennials, so everyone didn't get a prize).

JOHN HERBUT, Insurance

Writing Off What You Don't Know

"You're doing *what* on your smartphone?" "Wait, you're reading a newspaper made of *paper*?" If you're finding it hard to relate to someone from another generation, try keeping up to date on trends in your industry—this is something you can both connect on. Read articles (or hey, just keep reading and recommending this book!), stream an episode of the latest binge-worthy show, listen to a top podcast, or find really anything that could serve as a point of connection when chatting with your coworker. Don't know what this might be? Ask other people who speak that "language" for suggestions.

Keep It Quick

Studies show that Millennials have an attention span of twelve seconds, while Gen Z is down to just eight. To put that into perspective, a goldfish has an attention span of nine seconds.[4] It can be hard to communicate when the other person is already moving on to the next thing. Providing feedback in quick, easy, and digestible bites will go a long way. Find small chunks of time to have these conversations and avoid long-winded emails or conversations, unless absolutely necessary.

BE HUMAN. ACT HUMAN.

At the end of the day, people are people with unique experiences and viewpoints. Let's stop generation shaming—from "they're too old to understand technology" to "all Millennials are just lazy and don't know a thing about loyalty." Let's get to know the people we work with by asking them questions about their experiences, communication preferences, and motivations. The more we get to know people as people, the better our work culture will be.

CHAPTER 3

Having Real Conversations About Diversity, Inclusion, and Belonging

WE ALL HAVE biases. Whether we're conscious of them or not, they affect our interactions with others, how we make decisions, and our overall outlook on the future. In fact, our brains are hardwired to prefer certain things while feeling averse to others. This becomes an issue when we don't consciously recognize our biases and preferences. It's essential to accept that everyone, including you and me, has biases. Once we accept this, we can work on navigating what they are and how to handle them.

When the Unintended Still Hurts

Our viewpoints are based on a number of factors, including but not limited to

- Race and Ethnicity
- Family history
- Gender

- Generation
- Life experiences
- Religion
- Sexual orientation
- Socioeconomic status
- Values

When we make statements or act without taking others' viewpoints and values into consideration, we can offend and hurt them. Although potentially subtle, over time, these statements or actions—known as *microaggressions*—can do lasting damage by destroying relationships, by making people feel unwelcome, and by isolating them. Despite our best intentions, the overall impact our statements or actions make depends on how our audience perceives them.

I'll never forget a meeting several years ago with my peers and superior. We were having a conversation about diversity in the workplace. What it currently looked like, what it would look like in the future, and how diversity would impact our organization and beyond. My superior looked directly at me and said, "I see the map of Jerusalem all over your face." I was stunned, shocked, and didn't know what to say. The conversation moved on like nothing happened, and everyone around me stared, waiting for me to say something. I just looked down without speaking up and tried to forget it. As you can tell by my mentioning it now, it's a moment that stuck with me. It still affects me. Looking back, I see this as a missed opportunity for me to process my thoughts, to have an open discussion, or—at a minimum—to speak one on one with this person on how these words made me feel. I felt like I didn't have time to process my thoughts and decided it was better not to address it. This subtle, yet powerful statement made me feel isolated, insecure, and vulnerable. And my situation is not unique, although yours might not be as transparent.

HUMAN CONNECTION

I work for a medium-sized nonprofit with a very diverse staff. One of our Caucasian employees found a resource to help other Caucasians raise their awareness of internalized racism, an issue we have dealt with in our office. They emailed it to only the staff they perceived to be Caucasian.

Word quickly spread about the email and there were a range of emotions. Some non-Caucasian employees felt supported while others felt excluded. Other employees were upset because they were assumed to be Caucasian, when they were not. A few Caucasian employees felt singled out as if receiving the email implied they needed this resource.

As their manager, I met one on one with the employee who shared the information and explained the office feedback and the importance of sharing this type of material with all staff and not just a select few. I also personally sent a company-wide email that included the resource.

Although this person was trying to be helpful, they excluded employees in the process and made naïve assumptions. This lack of judgment led to an emergency meeting about inclusivity and affirmed the need to continue to bring in outside support to work through our microaggressive culture.

ANONYMOUS

Being able to create a workplace free of microaggressions and unintentional insults would be ideal, although not realistically achievable. However, reaching a place where people feel comfortable asking questions about our differences, with candor and respect, is also exceptional. We should be able to have open conversations without crossing lines or offending those around us—but that takes time and can feel challenging (and sometimes uncomfortable) to maneuver. As a workforce, we need to become aware of our unconscious biases and move forward to create a collaborative and inclusive environment. If we don't set out time and create opportunities for dialogue,

- Office gossip starts and spreads.

- Employees hold onto negative feelings about the people they work with.

- Unproductive confrontations occur.

- Employees avoid colleagues.

- Microaggressions continue and potentially increase due to lack of understanding.

As you approach this chapter, try to keep an open mind, as it will be a little different from the others you'll read in this book. We're going to break down vocabulary, share common and unintentionally harmful phrases, hear stories from employees who have felt marginalized, and walk through solutions and inclusive best practices across all types of differences.

As the diversity and inclusion landscape moves forward, we're no longer just talking about outright racism or sexism in our workplaces. It's much more nuanced. Diversity and inclusion initiatives and education are moving away from applying labels to everything (this is a training about race, this is an initiative around gender), and into an inclusive space that encompasses all types of diversity.

This chapter is not intended to spotlight one specific type of bias or employee. Instead, it frames our differences in race right alongside our differences in religion, life experiences, and so on. The goal is to become more self-aware of the language we use, know when and how to be an ally, and find ways to have constructive conversations with those who have unintentionally used hurtful language. We're all individuals and identify with multiple elements that make us who we are. We're not one dimensional and don't have one singular identity.

A lot of this is not easy to talk about, and the practices presented will take time to practice, vulnerability to execute, and empathy to be effective. We're all coming from different places in life. It's all about using our unique voices to free our workforces of microaggressions, one conversation at a time.

HUMAN CONNECTION

Whenever we encounter something, we can experience it as unpleasant (negative) and want to avoid or escape it or as pleasant (positive) and crave more of it. This concept is called *valence* and it is tied to two patterns of brain activity. In the Calm Clarity approach, we call them Brain 1.0 and Brain 2.0. Brain 1.0 is the fight-or-flight and avoidance system. It is activated when you experience something unpleasant or unsafe, and you want to avoid it. You are then going to associate that experience, object, or person with Brain 1.0 so it will self-activate in the future. This is called *conditional learning.* Similarly, Brain 2.0 activates when you experience something as positive and pleasant. Then when you see it again, your conditional learning response is to approach it.

Brain 1.0 and Brain 2.0 underlie bias. Your brain makes an assumption based on previous experiences on whether or not to approach or avoid certain people, objects, or experiences. Unconscious bias happens when we're not even aware that we have been conditioned this way and we make decisions we believe are rational that are actually based on preconditioning. In the 21st century, we're saturated with media images and news stories that depict stereotypes, and when we go to social events where we're exposed to other people's prejudices, we can absorb them and unconsciously associate one person with Brain 1.0 and another person with Brain 2.0.

In addition, our biological programs for out-group aversion and in-group favoritism go back to our caveman days. In those times, when someone from a group saw a stranger, the stranger was seen as dangerous because the group member didn't know what that person's intentions were. In general, people who looked like you were safer than people who didn't. As a result, we're actually hard-wired to activate Brain 1.0 when we meet people we perceive to be different from us and Brain 2.0 when we meet people we perceive to be like us. The activation of Brain 1.0 toward out-groups causes us to hold people in out-groups to higher standards. This means people in out-groups have to work twice as hard for us to believe they are safe, trustworthy, and reliable.

In organizations, when decisions are driven by Brain 1.0 and Brain 2.0 at a subconscious level without awareness, it can create limiting patterns, behaviors, and suboptimal results. The key to breaking these patterns is activating and strengthening a pattern of brain activation we call Brain 3.0, which corresponds to the neural networks for self-mastery and intrinsic motivation. We can activate Brain 3.0 using simple practices, such as visualizing what the highest expression of who we are looks like, and imagining what this higher self would say and do in any challenging situation we find ourselves in. Another practice is to set an intention to connect as human beings who need to be seen and heard with compassion and imagine speaking to the inner child in the other person.

DUE QUACH, CEO of Calm Clarity

Individualizing Inclusion

We each think, act, and experience life differently due to a variety of factors, including the ones we addressed earlier. Yet we still use the phrase "treat people the way you want to be treated." Although the sentiment is well intentioned, not everyone wants to be treated the way we do. This is missing a major component: the other person's preference. When we adjust our mindset to "treat people the way they want to be treated," we're being more inclusive and creating opportunities for open dialogue.

So, how can we find out the other person's preferences? We have to observe, have conversations, and build meaningful relationships. Embracing diversity helps us enhance creativity, give voice to varying backgrounds, and provide opportunities for unique problem solving. This can also translate into extending a client base or transitioning into new markets. According to McKinsey, ethnically diverse companies are 35 percent more likely and gender diverse companies are 15 percent more likely to financially outperform their national industry medians.[1]

HUMAN CONNECTION

If you want diversity, you need to hire diverse people. If a company is telling people they care about diversity and then you look at their website, their board of directors, or their executive team and don't visually see it, the message will fall on deaf ears. Employees take note of what their managers are doing just like kids do with their parents. If employees see leadership embracing and exhibiting microaggressive behaviors, they're likely to mimic it. If leaders say they care about diversity, they need to move past using buzz words and actually show that they do, starting with the hiring process. Companies need to make an effort to foster a culture of inclusion by either promoting people who are passionate about diversity to help the organization change or by bringing new people in.

DR. JANICE ASARE, Diversity and Inclusion Consultant and Professor

One of my clients was having issues with how their employees communicated with one another. Although some tended to take a more casual approach to language and would make jokes about their identity, others were not as amused. Phrases like, "I'm a redneck," were being thrown around the office to describe their upbringing and experience. Although the person identifying as a redneck saw no harm in this phrase, others within earshot were offended. So, although the phrase was not offensive to the person saying it, their coworkers with similar upbringings were uncomfortable with its use. Through ongoing conversations, the team was able to share why this phrase was offensive and make an active effort to be more conscious of their language choices. A definite shift was needed to "treat others the way *they* want to be treated." This was not something that happened overnight, and it took the courage and vulnerability of one person to initiate the conversation.

Here's a subtler (and common) example. As much as I appreciate being acknowledged for doing good work, I would be mortified to be called out in a large meeting about my accomplishments. I would prefer a one-on-one acknowledgement. If I treat others the way I want to be treated, I wouldn't acknowledge them in a public forum; rather, I would focus more on individual conversations. Although some may like this approach, others would not. Some employees may want the whole organization to know what they've done for the company and would feel slighted if I didn't take the time to let others know about their accomplishments. Now, instead of assuming others want to be treated the way I do, I ask the employee, "How do you like to receive praise?" This gives the individual the opportunity to clue me in to their personal preferences and for me to follow suit.

Navigating the Unfamiliar

Talking about our differences can be tricky, and most of us are uncomfortable with what we don't know. Let's say someone brings up a term or phrase that you're unaware of or discusses a holiday or tradition that you've not experienced. You could be thinking any number of things, like

- Should I already know this?
- Should I just stay quiet and not say anything?
- Should I pretend I already know and just smile and nod?
- Can I ask this person about this?
- If I do ask, what should I say and how can I say it without offending them or having them think I'm ignorant?

Staying quiet and avoiding asking questions can send the wrong message and lead to more miscommunications down the road. Instead of setting ourselves up for issues later on, we should be having more honest and open dialogue in a respectful way that shows we're interested in learning and understanding.

It can be hard to ask these questions of someone you don't have a close relationship with. Consider taking baby steps and asking a colleague you're closer with, or even a personal friend or mentor. Sometimes a quick Google search of the topic or question can give you some insight and help you feel more comfortable with the direction of your conversation. But before engaging in what could be a difficult dialogue, here are a few things to consider:

Avoid a one-size-fits-all mentality. No one wants to be the token person representing a race, ethnicity, gender, or disability. How one person feels or views something doesn't equate to everyone else feeling that way, too. The goal of this conversation is to be more inclusive by appreciating everyone as individuals. Try focusing on their personal experiences.

Ask permission. Before taking a deep dive into the conversation, make sure the person is comfortable having it. "Colleen, I'm interested in hearing your perspective and was wondering if you would be comfortable talking about it with me." Explain that you're interested in hearing about their personal experience and are not asking them to represent anyone but themselves. "This is not something that I have thought about before and I am wondering what your experience has been like."

If they're not interested in discussing this topic with you, drop the issue and find alternative resources. Do not push someone to talk about something if they're not comfortable with it. If you find yourself in this position, here are some alternative resources you can use to start your exploration:

- Visit national organization websites (i.e., National Association for Advancement of Colored People [NAACP], Anti-Defamation League [ADL], American Association of People with Disabilities [AAPD]).

- Explore best practices through articles and research from professionals (i.e., Society for Human Resource Management [SHRM], Association for Talent Development [ATD]).

- Take courses or watch talks by industry and research experts (i.e., LinkedIn Learning, TED, Coursera).

- Attend events with a focus on inclusion and supporting the growth of underrepresented communities (i.e., Hispanic Chamber of Commerce, Diversity and Inclusion conferences).

Understand that this is not a public discussion. Starting a discussion of this nature should be done privately and not in front of other colleagues, at a meeting, or in the hallway. Don't put the other person on the spot or call them out.

Come with an open mind. Let them know that you're genuinely interested in learning about their experiences and values. "Thank you for taking the time to talk with me about this. I really appreciate your sharing why gender-neutral bathrooms are important to you. I am interested in learning about this."

Avoid stereotypes. Although this might be obvious on the surface, it's important to not use derogatory language or stereotypes. If you know certain words fall into this category—don't use them. If you're unsure (or completely unaware) of whether something isn't OK to say, these conversations are crucial for you. When people are blind to the fact that statements are indeed derogatory, they continue to say them and perpetuate a microaggressive culture.

Have courage and be vulnerable. These conversations can be difficult and showing your vulnerability is a big step. Be brave and honest.

Respect boundaries. If you notice that the other person is uncomfortable with a question, don't keep pushing for an answer. Respect that they're taking the time to speak with you but might not be comfortable with all of your questions. Remember, this isn't an interrogation, it's a conversation.

HUMAN CONNECTION

When you're asking for days off or are being asked by an employee for days off for religious reasons, it's important to find mutual courage. No one likes to feel different, risk rejection, or ask for accommodations they feel could risk a promotion. Anything that makes us feel different is scary. As part of the ask, be ready to educate your supervisor. There is a presumption of knowledge, but many individuals are not aware of the significance of certain holidays and don't understand the needs of those who celebrate them. It's important to not just leave it as "I need to be out next Friday," but to take a few moments to explain what this holiday and tradition is and why you need the day off. You should also be ready for the questions about why you celebrate a specific holiday or tradition if your supervisor mentions they have a friend/colleague/acquaintance who does not celebrate it in the same way. Responding, "There is a diversity in every world religion and people practice differently. This is how I observe," would be an appropriate response. When we have these open conversations, it allows us to get a hopeful outcome.

REV. CHARLES HOWARD, PhD, Chaplain at the University of Pennsylvania

Now, let's say you're on the other end, and someone has asked you to have a conversation. Here are some things to consider:

You have the right to say no. If you don't feel comfortable with even beginning the conversation, you can politely decline the invitation. You're not under any obligation to engage in dialogue that you're not comfortable having. "I appreciate you asking me about this topic, however I don't feel comfortable discussing it. Thank you for understanding."

Choose the location. If a coworker has come to you to discuss something more personal, find a place where you feel comfortable, whether it's in one of your offices, a *huddle room* (small meeting room), or when taking a walk outside. "I would be happy to talk with you about this, let's head to our huddle room to continue the conversation."

Avoid a one-size-fits-all mentality. It's important to recognize that your perspective is not the perspective of everyone. You're not there to act as a representative of an entire race, religion, or identity group. This helps to clear the air and understand the limitations of the discussion. "I can share my experience with this, but I just want you to know that this is not reflective of everyone else within the population."

Be empathetic. It may have taken this person a lot of courage to ask you this question, and they may even be visibly uncomfortable talking about it. They are sharing their vulnerability by revealing that they don't know something and are asking you, someone they trust, the question.

End the conversation or take a break, if necessary. You have the right to end the conversation or to take a step away from it. If there are things you're uncomfortable with, let the other person know and take the time you need for self-care. "I need some time to think through this question. Are you available for lunch next Thursday to continue the conversation?"

TIPS FOR ENGAGING IN UNFAMILIAR DIALOGUE

✔ Ask for permission.

✔ Understand that this is not a public discussion.

✔ You have the right to say no.

✔ Be empathetic.

✔ Avoid a one-size-fits all mentality.

✔ Come with an open mind.

✔ Avoid stereotypes.

✔ Have courage and be vulnerable.

✔ Respect boundaries.

Get Comfortable with Being Uncomfortable

Now, let's shift gears. What happens when someone says something or acts in a way that offends you? Remember, it doesn't matter whether it was intentional or not. If it has bothered you, your feelings are real and should be valued. But knowing what to say and how to say it is the next big step.

One of the first things to think about is whether or not you want to engage in the conversation in the first place. A way to help determine this is to think about whether the interaction will get in the way of your ability to work with the other person.

If you believe it will, it's important to consider having this conversation, no matter how difficult it might be to start. For issues like sexual harassment or blatant racism, consider contacting your supervisor or HR. If you believe it's a misunderstanding, however, and that having this conversation can diffuse the situation, try these steps:

Take some time to process. Before engaging in a conversation, take a moment to breathe and process the situation. It's not always best to immediately address an issue. Whether it's for a few minutes or a full day, be sure to give yourself some time before moving forward.

If you have someone you trust, like a mentor, consider reaching out to them to process the issue, too, but make sure the conversation stays between the two of you. Being able to externally evaluate the situation with someone else will keep you level-headed and might help provide a structure for your dialogue. Running this by someone else is also a great baby step to gaining the courage to have the actual conversation. You can even write out talking points and areas you want to address and rehearse them in front of the mirror.

Assume the best intentions. Assume the other person meant no harm by what they said or did and that they were unaware of the impact of their words or actions. If this is the case, bringing this up with them is a great opportunity to make them cognizant of a bias they're completely unaware they have. Helping them be aware of this could benefit their future interactions with others. Also, when we assume everyone has the best intentions, these conversations are easier to have. "I assume you did not mean to be hurtful in any way, but I want to bring to your attention that I was offended by your comments."

Provide a neutral location. Finding a neutral space where you and your coworker are both comfortable will make a big difference.

This could be a local coffee shop, a huddle room, or a work café, as opposed to your office.

Set the tone. The key is to create an environment without distractions. Show them that you're giving them your undivided attention and are interested in having an open and honest conversation. Try to incorporate these concepts:

> *Acknowledge the value.* By starting the dialogue with appreciation, you show that you're invested in both the conversation and the relationship. "Thank you for taking the time to speak with me."

> *Show empathy.* We all come from different backgrounds and life experiences, and that impacts the way we see the world and the people around us. Take a step back from what you think you know and try to understand the situation from the other person's perspective.

> *Understand word choices.* Avoid accusatory language that suggests the other person intentionally did something wrong. Phrases to avoid are things like "You meant to" or "You knew that wasn't appropriate."

State the facts. To make sure you're both on the same page as to what the conversation is about, make sure you clearly establish the who, what, and where of the situation that took place. This isn't a game of Clue. You want everything to be out in the open so it's clear what you are talking about. Lay out the facts first. "At our meeting this morning, when I disagreed with your idea and made an alternative suggestion, you said I was being 'dramatic' and 'high maintenance' in front of our whole team."

Share your feelings and observations. Although you may know that others feel similarly about the issue at hand, this conversation is about your feelings only—it's not about generalizing for a group. Make sure to use "I" statements instead of broad-reaching comments. Only share observable behaviors to avoid making assumptions. What did you see or hear and how did it make you feel? Focus on explaining your feelings, not what you think was intended by their actions. "When you made these comments, I felt uncomfortable and singled out."

Offer suggestions for the future. As part of the conversation, provide suggestions for what they could do if this situation comes up again. "In the future, please refrain from using those terms."

Show appreciation. Even though the other person said something or performed an action that offended you, take a moment to thank them for having this conversation with you; doing so goes along way. It extends not only a professional courtesy but opens the door to future conversations. "Thank you for taking the time to talk with me about this. I appreciate your willingness to avoid this language."

Stay calm. It's possible the person you're speaking to won't react positively—they might respond with anger or categorically refuse to listen. Know that in this type of situation, no good will come of trying to push the person into a conversation. Assess their reaction and walk away if you need to. Then talk to your supervisor or HR about how to handle it from there.

HUMAN CONNECTION

Early in my career as a resident director at a college, I was the only black woman on the staff. My supervisor consistently made racially insensitive comments and jokes like, "Here come ebony and ivory," referring to me and a coworker. I felt uncomfortable, but I didn't know how to assert myself and address the situation. I knew the comments were wrong and were contributing to a harmful and hurtful environment without inclusion and community. But as a young professional, I let it slide for too long.

It took me until the end of my first year to find the courage to tell my boss how her comments, remarks, and jokes made me feel. After I brought it to her attention, she finally eased up, and she explained that she was unaware that they were offensive. She was using these phrases without realizing their impact on me and our team.

Sometimes people are genuinely unaware that they can come across as prejudiced or offensive. These are people that you can have a conversation with, and they can see your point of view and make a conscious effort to really change.

Everybody deserves a safe and comfortable work environment, and that can only happen if we address the issues directly and have open dialogue.

DARLA STILL, Rating Specialist, Department of Veteran Affairs

If you're the one being asked to have a conversation, here are some things to think about:

Listen. Actually listen to what the person is saying. If they're taking the time to have this conversation with you, this situation really affected them. You may not have realized that what you were saying or doing was offensive, so take this as a learning opportunity to listen with the intention of understanding.

Body language. Adjust your body so you're facing them and follow their cues. If they sit, you sit. If they're standing, you stand. Use head nods to acknowledge that you're paying attention. These adjustments show that you're giving them your undivided attention and value their opinion.

Validate. This doesn't mean you're necessarily agreeing with the person, but it does mean that you recognize their feelings and experiences. In these situations, it's not about agreeing, but acknowledging: "That's so frustrating, I can understand why you're upset."

Be vulnerable. It's OK to not know what to say or how to say it, and it's easy to get defensive in these situations. Being vulnerable lets the other person know that you're human and you're listening. "I am not sure what to say. But I want you to know that I am listening to what you're saying, and I appreciate that we are having this conversation."

Accept responsibility. Whether it was intentional or not, we need to accept responsibility for our actions if we have any chance of moving forward. This is not the time to question their story, interrogate their feelings, or make a joke about it. Any of those routes can easily make a person feel devalued and isolated. It's also not the time to provide a critical response that puts the blame back on them. "Grace, if you weren't so uptight, this wouldn't be an issue."

Instead try

- "I take full responsibility for making those comments. My intention was not to offend you and I apologize for doing so."

- "Thank you so much for your feedback, I didn't even realize that I did that. I apologize for my actions."

- "Thank you for bringing this to my attention, and I am sorry for offending you. Can you tell me more about why this phrase is offensive? I want to make sure I understand so I don't repeat this in the future."

Offer follow-up and support. The goal of these difficult conversations is not to sway people to one side or the other, but to come to a place of mutual respect. Sometimes we need to prioritize understanding over being understood. This is not about completely changing your perspective to match someone else's. It's about making an active effort to understand the people you are working and conversing with.

If we want to be productive, conversations should stay focused on the impact and not the intent. There might not be an immediate solution, but offering to continue the conversation will lead you down a path to finding one. With that said, we need to toe the careful line of finding a solution together versus offering unsought advice. Sometimes someone just needs to vent and feel heard.

Some great closings to your conversations can be

- "I'm always here if you want to talk."

- "Is there anything that I can do to help you?"

- "I found our conversation very valuable and I would like to keep the dialogue going. Would you be open to having lunch next Thursday?"

TIPS FOR ENGAGING IN DIFFICULT DIALOGUE

✔ Take some time to process.

✔ Assume the best intentions.

✔ Provide a neutral location.

✔ State the facts.

✔ Share your feelings and observations.

✔ Be empathetic and vulnerable.

✔ Offer suggestions for the future.

✔ Show appreciation.

✔ Listen and be aware of body language.

✔ Accept responsibility and offer follow-up and support.

Don't Be Afraid to Share Your Expertise

One of the more prevalent communication issues in the workplace is *privileged explaining*. This is when either someone of perceived power, influence, or dominant gender provides an explanation or shares an idea in a patronizing or condescending tone.

I've worked in male-dominated spaces where a woman's idea was often overlooked in favor of a male colleague's similar, sometimes less-researched and thought-out, idea. I've also been in situations in which I trained colleagues and months later, they approached me to train me on the same "new" information they discovered. These types of micro-aggressions perpetuate a culture in which people not only don't feel valued, but are missing opportunities for diverse innovation and collaboration. These types of microaggressions are not limited to just gender biases; they can be seen in any of the different viewpoints noted at the start of this chapter. If you're experiencing the situations we've already discussed or similar situations, try using the conversation methods discussed earlier to address this one on one with the individual involved. You can also try these ideas to get your opinions heard and show your expertise:

Support your concepts. If you're sharing an idea, give data and facts that support your insights. If this is something you're intimately familiar with, try starting off with phrases like "In my experience" or "When I ran a similar project in my previous role."

Ask an insightful question. If someone is trying to show you up on a topic you're an expert in, ask them a specific question that only people who are familiar with the content would know. This isn't to one-up them but to show that you understand the language and are able to keep up.

Add something to the conversation. If you've been cut off from finishing your idea or concept, try "Let me finish my point" or "I have something else to say." Find a tone that is a little stern but not aggressive.

Repeat your idea. If someone stole your idea and is trying to play it off as their own, build on it. Repeat the idea and then say, "here's what I am thinking about." And then share and show the strategy and tactics behind the concept you've been working on. This will show that this is something you're not only knowledgeable about, but something you have conceptualized beyond this meeting.

There's no doubt that this is not an easy thing to do. Starting these conversations is no small feat, and it's equally difficult being on the receiving end, finding out that you've offended someone. But people can't apologize or change their behavior if they don't even know it has been a problem. As hard as it may be, it is our individual responsibility to address these issues if we want things to change.

Remember, these suggestions are things to think about and mull over before having a conversation, but you can't predict what people are going to say or where exactly the discussion will go. There is no script—dialogue is fluid and changes. Start by processing your thoughts and getting support, and then practice if you're not ready to take the leap right away.

HUMAN CONNECTION

I am a petite Asian woman who grew up in New York since I was one. I went to an Ivy League school and I have my PhD in higher education. During my second week at my new job, I took the bus to campus. As soon as I walked onto the bus, an older Caucasian man greeted me with *ni hao.* This was unnecessary—I speak excellent English. I don't care what his reason was—it was offensive. I knew this horrible moment would come at some point in this new place. It always does. I just didn't realize it'd come quite so soon.

I walked into my office looking just a little tired and just a little sad. One of my colleagues asked me what happened. I told her and she looked at me with sad eyes and said, "I'm so sorry that happened to you. There are some people around here who are just ignorant. I'm sad that your day had to start out this way. Do you need anything?" I talked to her for a while, sharing my frustration at feeling distanced and bothered—constantly having to answer the "Where are you from?" "No, I mean, where are your parents from?" "No, I mean, what's your heritage?" "What are you?" "No, I mean, what's your nationality?" "No, I mean, what's your culture?" questions. She looked at me with sad eyes and listened.

I had a meeting with another one of my colleagues later in the day. I told her the same story and she looked at me with a blank stare and said, "I'm really surprised that happened to you. That sort of thing just doesn't happen here." I looked at her somewhat incredulously and said, "Well, it did. It just happened. And he got off the bus when I did, which means he works on campus. So, it does happen here." We didn't say anything more. Thinking back, I could've shared more stories to frame that one experience, but I didn't know my colleague or work environment very well, and I simply didn't have the energy in the moment.

> If you want to engage in more inclusive conversations, you have to listen and affirm others and their experiences, especially when they tell you about the challenging ones. It's hard enough for them to open up and share; don't make it even harder by questioning the legitimacy of their stories.
>
> *DR. HOI NING NGAI, Higher Education Administrator*

What's an Ally and How Can I Be One?

Let's say you observe something that doesn't sit right with you, or you believe a certain group is not being treated fairly. This might motivate you to become an *ally.* Just to be clear, an ally isn't someone who stays neutral, it's someone who makes a choice to get involved and actively show support. Standing up for someone or a group of people who feel marginalized is a good thing . . . if you go about it in the right way. But, when we take charge, make assumptions, and ask for accommodations for a certain population that we don't identify with, this can actually do more harm than good.

Let's first talk about this delicate line, and when it gets crossed. In one of my previous positions, a coworker of mine was out for several weeks and came back to work with a cane and a minor limp. He was on the operations side of the office and had responsibilities that often required lifting heavier boxes in the supply closet, setting up for events, and tidying up the kitchen area. I noticed he was struggling using two hands while holding the cane and a large box, and I stopped what I was doing to help. The next day I came into the office and started talking with his supervisor about things we could do to help make the job more accessible for him until he was healed. Well, boy was I wrong to do that. I completely overstepped, and my coworker was furious. I was trying to be his ally without asking if he wanted one, or even what he might need.

When I discussed this with my coworker, he explained he was still capable of doing his job within its normal time frame and needed to build up the strength to get back to his regular pace. He wanted to prove to himself and the company that he would not be limited in any way. Although he appreciated my help, he wanted to be a part of the conversation as to what type of help would work best for the different stages in his recovery. After I accepted responsibility and apologized, we were able to heal our relationship over time.

In another situation, one of my coworkers noticed I was struggling to reach my newly moved mailbox (height is not one of my strengths). I was on my tiptoes and was about the climb up a small shelf to grab my mail when she asked if I needed any help. I gladly accepted, as I knew my accident-prone self would most likely fall in the process. The next day she came up to me and asked if this was something that occurred often and if I wanted her support to speak to the office manager to rearrange the mailboxes, along with other hard-to-reach supplies in higher cabinets. Not only did I appreciate my colleague's support, but as an ally, she asked before moving forward. Instead of making an assumption, she wanted to know what I would need and if I wanted her to advocate for me. I asked if she could support me in moving the mailboxes but said that I was OK with the office supplies location, as there was a small step stool nearby. Although this gesture may seem small, this made a huge impact in the way I worked, and our relationship grew as result.

Allies are not expected to fix the problem, but they are there to offer their support in working toward a solution, or simply to offer their empathy. An *ally* is a person of one social identity group who stands up in support of members of another group (usually a nondominant group). Allies are critical to improving diversity, inclusion, and belonging in organizations. If you consider yourself an ally or are interested in being one, here are a few things to keep in mind.

Recognize your privilege. Privilege doesn't mean that you've never had to struggle for something, or that you have tons of money that you don't know what to do with. It's the freedom that you've experienced to not have to think about how others will treat you in certain situations just because of who you are. For example, because I am *cisgender* (defined in the glossary at the end of this chapter), I don't personally need to think about which public restroom I choose, since my outward appearance, my pronouns (she, her, hers), and my identity match one of the binary choices. For many other people, however, this is not the case.

To put it another way, many of us experience *tunnel vision*. We can focus on what's in front us while not even knowing what exists on either side because we're not experiencing it. This is not because we're not concerned; it's just that we don't experience everything that other people experience. Before we can be allies, we need to understand how our privilege can impact our perspectives and try to understand what other people are going through.

HUMAN CONNECTION

I had a great interaction with a Kindergarten class I visited for story time. I introduced myself as Mr. Coffey and a little kid raised their hand and asked, "Are you a boy or a girl?" And I just said, "I'm a boy, thanks for asking," and the child said, "Thanks! Are we going to read that book you have? Because I like that book!"

I think we can learn a lot from kids and how they approach these questions. Although it's not always appropriate to ask someone so directly, I really appreciate and respect how accepting young kids are.

In a group setting at work, I've volunteered my pronoun first and then asked others to share theirs. I've been in situations where I've been uncomfortably singled out by a group leader, while the rest of the group just let their pronouns and identity speak for themselves. If we're going to ask one person, it's important to ask everyone else in the room.

In a one-on-one setting, it's a chance to be more casual. "I'm [name], I go by [pronouns], how about you?" This gives the other person the chance to share if they choose.

> Once you know someone's pronoun, remember it. Practice it in a mirror if you have to. Don't gossip or speculate even if the pronouns sound weird or wrong. It's important to believe people when they tell you who they are.
>
> RED COFFEY, *Children's Librarian*

Support don't lead. As an ally, it's essential to listen in order to understand what the other person or group needs before you try to "help." As I mentioned earlier, I moved too quickly without understanding what my injured coworker needed (or didn't need) and didn't give him a voice to share if he wanted support. Remember, you haven't lived the life this person has and it's important to learn and observe, not assume.

Ask questions about their needs and listen to what they're saying with the goal of being able to summarize and confirm. Try using this statement to kick off your summarization:

- "What I am hearing is . . ."

At the end of your summary, try this phrase to bring it together and confirm the emotion they are going through:

- "And you're feeling . . ."

Show up when the cameras aren't flashing. If you want to support someone or a specific population, show up when no one's looking. It's not about being seen by the bigwigs but about the people you're supporting. Showing up for a major event that the higher-ups will be at is one thing, but it can be more effective to attend a small lunch-and-learn put together by an interest group. These types of smaller actions will help you gain credibility and trust within a community.

Support diversity and inclusion initiatives. Many organizations have diversity and inclusion initiatives and programming that focus on different genders, generations, sexual orientations, or races and ethnicities. These are usually open to not only people who identify with that group but to allies who want to support their missions. By attending events and meetings, and by sharing information you learn with others, you can spread their messaging and get others involved as well. An example of a way to be supportive is to be more inclusive with the holiday decorations that are displayed in the office. Think tree, menorah, kinara, and any other decor that employees use to acknowledge holidays they celebrate.

HUMAN CONNECTION

As the Associate Director of Corporate Relations at Temple University School of Tourism and Hospitality Management, I was tasked with gaining access, opportunities, and engagement to professional organizations. At the time, it was a new school and it was difficult to compete in a crowded field. The traditional roadmap was to attend and exhibit at conferences, but that was challenging with a small budget, an unknown brand, and limited staff.

I had to take a creative and productive approach by aligning the school with a commitment to multiculturalism. I then became engaged and supportive of diverse communities.

I recall my first Hispanic Hotel Owners Conference. I had tremendous anxiety about whether I would be able to successfully communicate, and as a result, I ended up misjudging the attendees. The experience was nothing like I imagined; not only was it enjoyable and informative, but I also made great connections. I was disappointed in myself and vowed to never make assumptions about others again.

Through the years, I've learned that in order to be an ally, it's important to make a conscious decision to put yourself in situations in which you will meet people of other cultures. This gives you the opportunity to ask questions and examine your own biases. Through these conversations, you can notice differences in communication styles and values. You may make a mistake along the way, but it's important to take the risk to start the conversation.

GREG DESHIELDS, Executive Director of PHL Diversity

TIPS FOR BEING AN ALLY

✔ Recognize your privilege.

✔ Support, don't lead.

✔ Show up when the cameras aren't flashing.

✔ Support diversity and inclusion initiatives.

BE HUMAN. ACT HUMAN.

Make no mistake that talking about these issues can be difficult and even emotional. But it's crucial for us as individuals to understand one another and come to a place where we can appreciate our differences. If we keep sweeping these issues under the rug, we're going to increase disengagement and push more and more people away from us and our company. We all have the opportunity to set an inclusive tone and be an ally. Understanding that we all have different values and experiences is the first step, but we have to show support and engage in uncomfortable conversations to move ourselves and our organizations forward.

Now that you've read this chapter, take the time to read the following glossary of terms compiled from similar lists from the United States Census Bureau; the Office of Multicultural Affairs at University of Massachusetts, Lowell; the Office of Diversity, Inclusion, Equity, and Community Engagement at The George Washington University; The Avarna Group; and Scripps College. Knowing terms can be helpful, not only as you read the remainder of the text, but also as you discuss these nuanced topics at your organization or elsewhere. This is not a comprehensive list, and there will always be new terms and identifications, but this is a solid start.

Glossary of Terms

Ally: A person of one social identity group who stands up in support of members of another group; typically, a member of dominant group stands beside member(s) of a targeted group; e.g., a male arguing for equal pay for women.[2]

Bias: Prejudice; an inclination or preference, especially one that interferes with impartial judgment.[3]

Cisgender: Someone who feels comfortable with the gender identity and the gender expressions and expectations assigned to them based on their physical sex at birth.[4]

Classism: Prejudiced thoughts and discriminatory actions based on difference in socioeconomic status, income, and/or class.[5]

Color Blind: The belief in treating everyone "equally" by treating everyone the same; based on the presumption that differences are, by definition, bad or problematic, and therefore best ignored (i.e., "I don't see race, gender, etc.").[6]

Disability: A long-lasting physical, mental, or emotional condition. This condition can make it difficult for a person to do activities such as walking, climbing stairs, dressing, bathing, learning, or remembering. This condition can also impede a person from being able to go outside the home alone or to work at a job or business.[7]

Discrimination: Actions, based on conscious or unconscious prejudice, that favor one group over others in the provision of goods, services, or opportunities.[8]

Diversity: The concept of diversity encompasses acceptance and respect. It means understanding that each individual is unique, and recognizing our individual differences. These can be along the dimensions of race, ethnicity, gender, sexual orientation, socioeconomic status, age, physical abilities, religious beliefs, political beliefs, or other ideologies. It is the exploration of these differences in a safe, positive, and nurturing environment. It is about understanding each other and moving beyond simple tolerance to embracing and celebrating the rich dimensions of diversity contained within each individual.[9]

Ethnicity: A group of people who identify with one another based on a shared culture.[10]

Gender: The socially constructed concepts of masculinity and femininity; the "appropriate" qualities accompanying biological sex.[11]

Gender Expression: The external display of gender, through a combination of dress, demeanor, social behavior, and other factors, generally measured on a scale of masculinity and femininity.[12]

Gender Identity: Internal perception of an individual's gender and how they label themselves.[13]

Inclusion: Active, intentional, and ongoing engagement with diversity—in people and in communities (e.g., intellectual, social, cultural, geographic) with which individuals might connect.[14]

Microaggression: A subtle and unintentional discriminatory comment or action toward a minority or other marginalized group that reinforces a stereotype.[15]

People of Color: A collective term for men and women of Asian, African, Latin, and Native American backgrounds, as opposed to the collective "White" for those of European ancestry.[16]

Personal Identity: Our identities as individuals, including our personal characteristics, history, personality, name, and other characteristics that make us unique and different from other individuals.[17]

Prejudice: A preconceived judgment about a person or group of people, usually indicating negative bias.[18]

Privilege: A right, license, or exemption from duty or liability granted as a special benefit, advantage, or favor.[19]

Racism: Prejudiced thoughts and discriminatory actions based on difference in race/ethnicity.[20]

Race (versus ethnicity): Race is a false construct that historically and currently conflates skin color and ancestry with behavior and culture. However, though race is a false construct, its existence is a widely held assumption and has real consequences for all people.[21]

Safe Space: An environment in which everyone feels comfortable in expressing themselves and participating fully, without fear of attack, ridicule, or denial of experience.[22]

Sex: Biological classification of male or female (based on genetic or physiological features), as opposed to gender.[23]

Sexism: Prejudiced thoughts and discriminatory actions based on difference in sex/gender; usually by men against women.[24]

Stereotype: Blanket beliefs and expectations about members of certain groups that present an oversimplified opinion, prejudiced attitude, or uncritical judgment. They go beyond necessary and useful categorizations and generalizations in that they are typically negative, are based on little information, and are highly generalized.[25]

Transgender: Appearing as, wishing to be considered as, or having undergone surgery to become a member of the opposite sex.[26]

Transparency: Authentic and honest communication with stakeholders.[27]

Unconscious Bias: Discriminatory judgement and bias that we are unaware of. Our brain triggers it automatically and makes quick judgments and assessments of people and situations, influenced by our background, cultural environment, and personal experiences.[28]

PART II

Communication Styles Matter

CHAPTER 4

Opening Communication, Breaking Down Silos

ONE OF THE BIGGEST SILOS in an organization is in job functional areas. These *silos* are the spaces where all the members of a team are doing the same type of work, and as a result, they sometimes forget that other teams exist. Often, in larger companies, employees from one team don't interact with employees from another unless they need something. For example, a team might keep to itself except when there's an ask involved (like project funding, additional staff, or technology support).

These silos become even more distinct when a company is spread out on different floors or different sections of a building or when a portion of the company works remotely. In such cases, people don't have as much of a chance of running into each other in the halls or at the printer. As a result, when a task needs input from other departments, employees in silos find themselves not knowing how or who to ask to move forward. A team existing in a silo may have no idea of the time or effort required for a process being done by another team. Some employees might not even know that there are resources or people available to help them outside of their silo—resulting in wasted time and repeated efforts. In addition, these silos can lead to turf wars because employees don't know what other departments are working on and find themselves battling for who should own a project or have access to resources.

Like many societies, businesses tend to be siloed and segmented. This feeds our human need for structure and order. However, if we can't communicate with individuals in the next department over, what are we missing out on? What vital information are we missing that could help us stand out as leaders, employees, and an organization?

Let's say you work in sales for a company that designs and manufactures equipment. How often are you talking to the people who—you know—actually *manufacture* the equipment? The ones who work the floor to build it and who could probably explain its innerworkings in their sleep? Or what about the customer service reps on the frontlines, answering the phone calls and complaints from current and prospective customers? They're on the daily pulse of what is making customers happy and not so happy. If we don't ask them for their feedback and listen when they give it, how will we ever know what we're leaving out of the big picture?

This type of disconnect is happening across industries, whether you're selling equipment or treating a patient. And these divisions aren't just happening by department.

The Silo Effect

During the interview process for a role in higher education, I was given the opportunity to meet with several teams to identify if I would be a good fit for the organization. They each shared the exciting projects and events they were working on and what was coming down the pike. I noticed that a few of the events they were mentioning were similar in purpose and were taking place on the *same* day and time. They were essentially competing with one another to get the same students at separate events. It became clear to me that not only did the departments not work together to meet their organization's larger goals, but they were also unaware that they were duplicating efforts.

After noticing the ongoing overlap in these conversations, I started to ask questions about working across departments. "Can you share examples of when various departments worked together to achieve a goal?" "What is your biggest challenge working in a siloed organization?" "How do you identify what department is tasked with a specific part or entirety of a project?" "How often do your departments get together to discuss what you're working on and how you can support one another?" I never thought I would see such confused faces after what I thought were simple questions about working together.

While listening to their answers, I was imagining money being wasted, employee workloads overextending, and a turf war about to explode. If I was hired, I knew one of my biggest goals was going to be to try to open the lines of communication within the organization. For this organization to survive and thrive, they had to work together. After I was offered and accepted the job, I took a step back to identify the landscape before making any of the moves that we talk about in this chapter. In a new job, it's important to give it some time and lots of thought rather than coming in hot with a big list of changes.

If you also find yourself spotting a lack of communication across departments or teams during an interview, take that into consideration when deciding whether it's an organization you want to work for. Although bringing people together is something I enjoy doing, I recognize it's not everyone's cup of tea. It can be hard work and requires a nuanced approach. Take note if this is a red flag for you and make your decisions accordingly.

I believe that every department in an organization needs the others to function, whether the organization realizes it or not. Creating strategic partnerships and shared space for ongoing conversations is essential. However, the time to start these conversations isn't after a situation happens or a problem arises. Start talking before such a situation even starts. Being proactive helps build trust and a culture of service, and it shifts the dialogue from "we need you to do something for us" to "how can we work together for the best interest of the organization?" It also enhances collaboration while decreasing duplicate efforts.

HUMAN CONNECTION

Our human services nonprofit was very siloed, and as part of our effort, we created opportunities for cross-collaboration. We established a training steering committee and development, delivery, and learning management system subgroups. These groups have representation from all departments and meet monthly or quarterly. They discuss all training issues and initiatives being developed to see if they can be used in more than just one division.

These efforts have made a huge difference for our organization. As opposed to creating a policy, training, or initiative for only one department, we're now able to implement programs that benefit the entire organization. This way of organizing our business also gives a voice to our frontline employees so they can share their ideas with upper-level leadership. Instead of creating a culture of "no," we created a culture of "yes and" where ideas are now built on top of other ideas.

DREW ALBERT, Manager of Culture and Development

Collaboration: Move Past the Buzzword

Collaboration is a word that gets thrown around a lot, and in some cases, it has lost its meaning due to overuse. We assume that if we tell our supervisors we're *collaborating* or share with our employees that *collaboration is important*, that we're on the same page on what it actually means. In some organizations, even saying the words *let's collaborate* leads to eyes rolling across the room. For some employees, this just sounds like, "Here's more work."

So, let's start off by talking about what collaboration is, and more importantly, what it isn't. You'll most likely see this word in one form or another in your company's mission statement. It may also show up as *teamwork* or *partnership*. In its essence, business *collaboration* means working with others to produce something. It's a two-way street where all parties involved are sharing knowledge and actively participating in the mutually beneficial relationship. Collaboration isn't when one side does all the work and you both take credit, or when you just simply share information or push work onto someone else. True collaboration is when both parties are invested and working together.

But this is not something that can just happen on its own or in a vacuum. It requires an understood company culture, a defined system, and the appropriate resources and tools that encourage employees to work together across departments. When collaboration works, it not only helps the company's bottom line, but it also enhances morale, development among the staff, and communication across functional teams.

Although some of the areas we'll talk about in this chapter fall under collaboration, it's important not to use this as an umbrella term any time people have a conversation across departments. When we generalize it, that's when we lose the essence, or worse, it starts getting used as a guise for passing the buck. "Wow, I'm really not into this project. Maybe I can 'collaborate' with Ted . . ."

Instead, we're going to focus on how to open the lines of communication in order to lead to real, effective collaboration. This approach can also lead to actively sharing information and creating a better understanding of the roles and responsibilities of employees.

HUMAN CONNECTION

I once led a team with five direct reports with different roles and team responsibilities. They had varying backgrounds, skills, personalities, and years of experience.

We worked together on several assignments, including one to introduce new operational reporting metrics to our organization. By the time this assignment was initiated, the team was already working well together. Our team meetings were upbeat, and conversation typically spanned a mix of work-oriented and light-hearted topics (e.g., current events, sharing of personal stories, etc.). It was never forced or contrived, but rather it came very naturally. When disagreements arose during the assignment, it was never personal; everyone listened openly and challenged each other to build their understanding or resolve their disagreement.

We had prior experience that our collective work products were viewed very positively by our leadership and we knew that no one person in our group had the answer. My team would constantly joke that I actually *knew* the answer but would keep it to myself so that they could come up with it on their own. In part, this was true. But this team thrived by arriving upon solutions—they did not want to be told the answer, because they enjoyed being creative. As a result, their work product was often far greater than anything I had personally conceived.

C. COFFEY, VP of a Large Insurance Company

Lead (and Communicate) by Example

As with many things in an organization, conscious support from the top can create an organizational shift in how we view cross-department communication. If leaders are not only saying that they value collaboration, but are demonstrating it by working with other departments, real change can start to happen. That means that leaders are proactively asking questions about other areas' needs, actively listening to these concerns, and working with one another to create a solution.

HUMAN CONNECTION

One way the technology landscape has changed is through "freemium" plans offered by companies like Slack and Box. With these free plan options to choose from, employees who are not the IT decision makers are given the opportunity to select and use the technology that works best for them.

We're in a time when the people with the problem can be the ones making the decision. This can easily be done on a team-by-team basis. If you're in a 2,000-person company, your 20-person department can opt for these solutions to internally share documents.

Employees can and will make technology decisions without IT. And ultimately, any problems with their technology will ultimately become IT's problem anyway. So, it's important for IT departments to make sure they're staying on the pulse of what their employees want and are communicating openly with them about their needs. Why not work with them to provide solutions up front than work backward after problems start happening?

JUAN VASQUEZ, VP of Engineering at Modsy

With all that said, willing leaders are not always enough. Employees often don't share information because they

- Lack the time

- Like being the expert or go-to person and want to ensure job security

- Are not rewarded for doing so

- Were never asked

A culture that values communication across teams needs to debunk these excuses and provide support and resources. Let's tackle a few ways that leaders can start to bring people together from different departments.

Collaborate Then Compensate

As we're talking about the importance of working across departments, it can be hard to see how this might actually work, or why employees would even try. We tend to set up recognition, reward systems, compensation, and promotions based on individual performance. This can be viewed as in direct conflict with the collaborative culture we're trying to establish. In most companies, performance reviews are typically about how we performed as individuals during the review period and not about how our team or group of teams did.

If your organization has a formal review where you're ranking competencies, consider adding cross-department collaboration to the list. How did they help another team move forward? What was their contribution to the success of the group? If it's something employees are evaluated on, and their paycheck is tied to how well they perform, it can help push the needle forward.

HUMAN CONNECTION

I like individuals who voice their opinion (good, bad, or ugly), because at least you know they have a pulse. It's important to share it in commentary (written or verbal) about policies, initiatives, programs, and things the company is doing. Feedback alone is a great indication of engagement. When it happens in reviews, it's more calculated and "check-the-box," and it is important to find ways to get more informal feedback. We need to make sure we're walking the walk and gauge how people show up in a number of different ways.

To do this, we created voluntary engagement teams across departments, locations, and functional areas where we actively solicited feedback on leadership, communication, values and direction, and service initiatives. The team's suggestions led to the CEO having breakfast with another department every 30–45 days without management present to encourage more candid conversations. It also led to the creation of our company's shared commitments. These commitments were rolled out by the CEO during a kickoff event and are now integrated into our performance reviews. Twenty percent of the reviews focus on how employees live out their shared commitments. They are also part of the company-wide rewards and recognition program, displayed on office banners and on vinyl laptop stickers. To ensure its success, we have also asked managers to keep these values front and center in team conversations. Although there is risk in soliciting feedback, it is risk worth taking.

RHONA FROMM, Vice President of Human Resources for Almo Corporation

Cross-Team Conversations

It's important to be intentional and create spaces and opportunities to understand what other departments are responsible for and how their work impacts the overall success of your team's projects, organization, and clients.

In one of my previous higher education roles, we proactively set up a cross-department meeting. My department focused on the academic side—helping students with courses and selecting their major—and residence life oversaw where the students lived. Both of our departments felt very disconnected from the other part of our students' lives and wanted to gain a better understanding of each other's roles to better assist our undergraduates. We also worked across a very large campus and rarely, if ever, saw each other.

To combat this, we held a meeting with both teams twice a year where we focused on updates, upcoming deadlines, and things to look out for. In between these meetings, a representative from both departments would attend the other department's monthly meeting and report back to their team. This gave all of us the opportunity to understand the academic cycle of events and helped us find better ways to work with one another to support our students. It also helped us establish who was responsible for specific tasks and gave everyone a contact person from the other team. After the first joint meeting, we started to collaborate more. Instead of residence life creating one program on choosing a major and our department creating another, we worked together to identify the common questions we were all hearing and created one cohesive program.

Consistency and established frequency are the keys to creating this kind of cross-departmental liaison system. Attending one or two meetings from another functional area may give you some information, but it does not help build relationships or open the lines of communication. It also does not give you a better grasp of the flow of a project from beginning to end. By having a year-round representative attend the residence life meetings, we were able to better understand their busy times and plan accordingly. Creating spaces where you either attend other departments' meetings or establish a joint meeting can be the start to collaborating across teams.

The goal is to create a space where teams have a mutual understanding that you're there to support one another and not to start a turf war. You can do this by asking strategic and clarifying questions during these sessions like these:

QUESTIONS	BENEFITS OF ASKING THE QUESTION
"What initiatives or large-scale projects is your team working on right now?"	This will help you see if there is overlap in the work you're doing and can be a primer for a larger discussion on how best to work together.
"Are there any upcoming deadlines we should be aware of? We want to make sure we're being respectful of your workloads."	By asking this question you can better space out your requests and understand why it may take longer for a response at different times of the month or year.
"As we're looking forward to next quarter, is there anything that my team can do to support your team?"	This helps you gauge not only what is coming up but it also shows you're a team player and are interested in working and supporting their team.
"Have there been any issues lately where you were not made aware of who to contact from our department? I want to make sure you're not put in a position where you don't know who to reach out to with questions."	This shows that you want to be transparent with the responsibilities of your team to ensure their team is successful.

Roles, Responsibilities, Transparency

Have you ever had a question and didn't know who to ask? It's hard to be collaborative if you don't even know what other people in your organization are responsible for. When you don't work directly with other departments or areas within your company, it can be difficult to figure out who does what. Titles are usually vague and don't give descriptions about the specifics of someone's day to day.

As a manager, you might know what each of your employees does, but perhaps you have not made it a point to share their specific roles with the larger group. And although it's great that you know if everyone isn't on the same page, it can lead to confusion and headaches. "Wait, so if Lonnie doesn't know, who do I ask now? Brianne? Doreen? Both?" This is especially important if you manage more than one team that does not interact on a daily basis but only comes together for project-based work.

We need to be more transparent about our roles and responsibilities. When we share what we oversee, tasks we complete, resources we provide, and what institutional knowledge we bring to the table, it makes life easier for everyone involved. Without that kind of information sharing, there is serious risk of duplicating efforts and longer lead times to get answers. "There have been so many moving parts lately, and I wanted to take a few moments with our team to share what I'm working on right now, what's coming down the line, and what information other departments come to me for. I'm hoping this will help if someone from another department reaches out and you're not sure who does what."

Clarity Is a Good Thing

Having a clear sense of what is expected of each employee is a win for everyone. For example, Tanya might ask Justin to order office supplies, while Julie asks Ethan for the same thing. If Justin and Ethan aren't working together, and Tanya and Julie don't clarify who's going to ask for what, you've now purchased twice as many supplies as you need. And you've also spent twice as much time researching the best price and placing the order. This is a simple example, and it will not solve all overlap issues, but if everyone knows that Ethan orders the supplies and Tanya does the inventory, Julie knows she doesn't have to worry about it. And you've increased your efficiency.

So how do you start hashing out all this clarity? Let's start by asking individual employees. Yes, we may have the job description they were hired under, but this may not be reflective of what they're actually doing in their job. So, go to the source.

Remember, though—if you're asking people to clarify their role, it's also important to provide them with context along with your request. Simply saying, "Ethan, please send me a list of your job responsibilities," might send Ethan into a panic. "Am I doing something wrong? Do they think I don't do enough? Am I getting fired?" If you're the one asking for this information, put the person at ease—share why you need it and that you value their work. "We're putting together a company list with all employees and their roles and responsibilities. We've received feedback that employees want to know who to reach out to for specific questions, and our hope is this fluid directory will be the start to this solution. We recognize the value of your role here and want to provide everyone with a resource of contacts to save you time and potential frustration when troubleshooting problems and working through projects."

Some employees might be afraid to share what they do. They might feel like they're being pressured or put on the spot. They can feel like they are being accused, as if they need to justify what they're doing all day. If you encounter this with an employee, continue to reinforce the value they bring and how it's important for you to share this with their teammates. Give them the time they need to process and respond. And if this reaction sounds like one you yourself might have as an employee, know that sharing what you do will help ensure that the job is done right so that you don't have to recheck or redo someone else's work. It will save you time in the long run. Don't let your ego or fear of losing your job get in the way.

HUMAN CONNECTION

In preparation for an employee taking a vacation or short-term leave, I proactively schedule a one-on-one meeting. During this conversation, I ask them what they're working on, the timeline for this work, and who else is involved in the process. This conversation is not always easy. My employees feel ownership for their projects and are confident they can complete the necessary tasks before they leave and give direction for when they're away. Because of this, I can get pushback on why I need this information in the first place.

Through the years, I've learned to stress that I want to set them up for success for when they return, and my intention is to keep them informed on the progress in their absence. I make it more about them enjoying their time away and less about needing the information. From there, we work together to create Google docs to share relevant information, and I copy them on all email communication when they're away. I make it clear that I'm only copying them on emails so they can be informed of the chain of dialogue and that I do not expect them to respond. Our proactive conversations, shared documents, and consistent communication has helped my employees pick up where they left off as soon as they get back. They can follow the email string and see where the project is without feeling completely lost. I also preschedule a one-on-one meeting upon their return to tie up any loose ends.

DEBBIE ROMAN, *Vice President of Membership and Community Engagement for Girls Scouts of Greater New York*

Use a Shared Tool to Map Out Roles

When you are putting all of this information on roles and responsibilities together, realize that it doesn't have to be some complicated org chart or contain fancy graphics. It can be a simple list of who does what, a quick description of what they can help out with, and their contact information. Keep in mind that this information should be easy to access, updated frequently, and available to the entire organization.

Try using a shared application or cloud-based platform that can be accessed from anywhere by more than one person at a time. Encourage users and managers to review and update this information on a consistent basis. You can even send monthly or quarterly reminders and make it part of the task list for newly hired or promoted roles. Having an outdated chart with people who've left the company months ago might be worse than not having one at all. So, it is important to keep it fresh and treat it as a living document.

Show Appreciation Across Departments

Once you've started to open the lines of communication across areas, it's important to keep the momentum going. In order to do that, you have to share the value of working with one another.

One of my favorite things to do at work or in my personal life is to reach out to someone's boss and let them know how awesome their staff are. I call customer service lines for retail stores to rave about a store clerk, and I love to ring those fun "thank you" bells after checking out with an awesome employee. At work, I'm always sure to email the supervisors of my collaborators from other departments and give them a specific example of how this person went out of their way to help me and my team.

Too often, we spend too much time complaining and not enough time thanking people. You never know if this will lead to a promotion or recognition for this individual. (Talk about a small way to make a big difference in someone's day!) Whether you're the leader of the group or not, you can take a moment to appreciate someone else's contribution, and if the praise is coming from another department, it can have even more of an impact. "Maria was such an asset on this project. She spent time helping all of us understand your team's sales cycle and has provided helpful suggestions to consider as we move to a cloud-based platform." The person you're reaching out to isn't your boss, and you have nothing to gain from showing appreciation. You're genuinely doing it to share how their work has positively impacted your team.

To take it one step further, if you want to thank another team for their collaboration on a project, invite them to lunch, host a happy hour, or give a gift card to those who went above and beyond. Above all, don't forget to say "thank you" either in person or through a note. And when I say note, I don't mean an email. I'm talking about an actual *handwritten* note! Unwrap that stationary your mom gave you two birthdays ago and start using it.

Send a note to an employee in another department who stayed late working with your team or drop off a card to a peer who answered when you called in a favor to help your team meet their sales goals. Appreciate people and say thank you. Kind little gestures like this can increase morale in the overall company and willingness to work together in the future. If we don't see that we're appreciated for our work in other departments, we'll go back to our silos and it will be harder to get us back out.

Collaborate, Win, Repeat

When your team has successfully collaborated with another team, shout it from the rooftops! Let everyone at the next company-wide meeting see how you worked together. The positive outcomes may include customer engagement, decreased expenses, and completing a project ahead of schedule. When people can see increased profits, sales, and a better customer experience, collaboration becomes more than just a buzzword; it becomes a motivator for stepping up and working together. And it shows what true collaboration really looks like. So, when your manager says, "I think we should collaborate with the marketing department on this project. Their experience in engaging with our target customer can help us make more informed decisions on our new chat platform," you can now envision what this collaboration might look like.

In sharing these successes, you can also recognize high performers and team players by name so people can become more familiar with the positive impact they made for your group. Although you might be involved in the project, you're not apt to be familiar with everyone's input; your other team members may have worked with someone else more closely. When giving recognition, to ensure you didn't miss anyone in another area, ask your team, "What contributions from other departments would you like to recognize?"

BE HUMAN. ACT HUMAN.

Bringing people together across departments requires intentional effort and modeling from the top. Leaders need to be open to collaboration to foster this culture in their teams. Leaders also need to be able to provide an answer to "What's in it for me?" Employees need to see the value-add for this to work. Sharing knowledge is a good thing and it leads to good results—better sales, awesome products, new solutions. Collaboration is not just a buzzword coming down from management, it really is the way we need to be working, today and into our future. It will make our teams stronger and our individual gains even more rewarding.

CHAPTER 5

Making the Most of In-Person Meetings

MEETINGS, MEETINGS, AND MORE MEETINGS. One thing that I hear from clients, regardless of what company or industry they represent, is how frustrated they are with the number of unproductive meetings they are required to attend. Our natural default way of disseminating information is to get people together—virtually or in person. According to the Association for Psychological Science, employees are in an average of six hours of meetings per week.[1] And for managers, it's even more: 23 per week! That's 300+ hours for employees and almost 1,200 for managers a year! Do you know how much that's costing your company?

Let's start by figuring out how much it's costing one of your employees with a salary of $50,000 a year:

- $50,000/1,853 (number of hours worked per year assuming four weeks of vacation and holidays[2]) = $26.98 (per hour)

- $26.98 × 6 (number of hours per week in meetings) × 48 weeks per year = $7,771 (total cost of salary spent in meetings)

Now let's take a look at a manager who is making $75,000 a year:

- $75,000/1,853 hours (number of hours worked per year assuming four weeks of vacation and holidays) =$40.47 (per hour)

- $40.47 × 23 (number of hours per week in meetings) × 48 weeks per year =$44,684.30 (total cost of salary spent in meetings)

To put this into perspective, if you're having a one-hour meeting with seven people (one manager and six employees with salaries comparable to those just listed), you're spending $202.35 per meeting. If you ask me, that's a lot of money and time to spend on putting people together just to share updates that could be sent via email. So how do we make the best use of our time, while still building relationships and maintaining clear communication? By being more intentional and not having as many unnecessary meetings.

Of course, there are still going to be times and circumstances when we need meetings. They help us gather authentic feedback, engage in powerful discussions, and provide us with an opportunity to get to know one another. The key is to make sure we're maximizing the limited time we have and that we are making sure people feel valued and heard.

Who *Really* Needs to Be There?

One of the most important areas to think about is who you need to invite. It's not about the quantity of people, but the relevancy of their role to what's up for discussion. Focus on having the appropriate decision makers in the room. I can't tell you how many meetings I've been to where the right people weren't there, and we had to hold additional in-person meetings because we didn't have the information we needed to proceed. Or the meetings I've attended where we talk about future meetings where the right people will be there. Let's just say there were always a lot of eye rolls, frustrated faces, and gossip after those sit downs, which was a symptom of employees being angry at and losing trust in those leading these pointless conversations.

Full disclosure, I've also scheduled meetings where I didn't want to leave anyone out, so I not only invited the key players but included a lot of spectators. I was afraid people would be offended if they weren't invited, even though their roles weren't directly related to the project we were working on. The key players were annoyed because there were just too many voices in the room, and the spectators felt like it was a waste of their time. There can be a delicate tight rope to walk to find the right balance of who should and shouldn't be sitting at the table.

Before you schedule any meeting,

Think about the reason you're having one and what information you want to share or discuss. Are you reviewing the whole project from start to finish, focusing on a certain issue, or is it a general update?

Identify the key players in this scenario and create your attendee list. As a general rule of thumb, keep it to a maximum of two people per department or area to avoid unnecessary representation.

TO NARROW DOWN THE GROUP, THESE PEOPLE SHOULD HAVE ONE OR MORE OF THE FOLLOWING ROLES:	TO CLARIFY THEIR ROLE AND NECESSITY, ASK YOURSELF THESE QUESTIONS:
▪ Power or authority to make decisions ▪ Ability to move things forward ▪ A specific area of expertise that applies to this project In addition, the outcome of this meeting has an impact on them or their team.	▪ If this person couldn't come, would I need to cancel the meeting? ▪ Who do I need in the room to get results and move this project forward? ▪ Who has institutional knowledge of this project and will bring necessary value and experience to this discussion?

Send out the invitation to those you've solidified are vital. The invitation should include

- Agenda

- Information you need from attendees prior to the meeting with a due date

- Their role within the context of this meeting (i.e., sharing department updates)

- Prereading or review material (i.e., stats, press release)

- Note indicating a back-up person is required if the recipient cannot make it (if applicable)

Nolan,

Our company's revenue meeting will be held on Thursday, January 5, in Conference Room A. I have attached the agenda. Please feel free to email me directly with additional items at least two days before the meeting.

Please bring your team's sales report and be prepared to discuss where you are with meeting your year-end goals and what support you may need from other departments to meet the goal. If you're not able to join this meeting, please let me know who will be representing your department in your absence.

Warm Regards,
Sebastian

Remember that your attendees don't need to be present for the whole meeting if all of the content doesn't apply to them. Consider inviting them to the beginning to share their information and then give them the option to leave early, specifying this in your invitation. I can promise you that they will greatly appreciate it!

Identify Your Why

Before any meeting, send out an agenda. Not five minutes before the meeting starts, but a good 48 to 72 hours ahead, if possible. Give the team the heads up about exactly what you're going to talk about. Then break the meeting into different sections, noting the focus of each agenda item:

Information sharing	Upcoming projects, company announcements, new information, or reminders
Feedback	When someone on the team has an idea they would like to share and are looking for others to brainstorm and provide input
Discussion	Anything that requires an open conversation

Giving everyone the heads up on not only what you're talking about, but also why you want to talk about it, goes a long way. If you find that your meeting is all information sharing: *cancel it!* Put all this information in an email, text, singing telegram, you name it—however you want to share this info in a way that doesn't require putting everyone in a room together. Very few people want to sit there and listen to you talk about something they can easily read over at their desks. A meeting that could have been an email is a recipe for frustration.

If there's a lot of brainstorming to be done, give people the opportunity to pre-brainstorm. Not everyone can think on the spot, and they may feel threatened in a meeting if ideas don't come to them easily without preparation. Give these prompts to folks in the agenda beforehand so they can think about them internally before meeting with the group. This is a great way to even the playing field for those who think in different ways (remember our strengths chapter), and it will result in more insightful feedback.

You can also give specifics as to what type of feedback you're looking for. Are you looking for alternative methods? Potential clients? Timelines? Procedures? Give your attendees some time and the information they need to be able to help you move your idea forward. This goes for anyone in any role, not just team leaders. If you want feedback, it's more effective to ask for it. If you want people to know what's going on in a meeting, you need to give them ample time to review the agenda!

Team,

I am looking forward to our meeting in two weeks. In preparation, I have attached our agenda and have noted the specific areas we will be discussing. There is one particular item that I would like to spend a significant amount of time on, the Atlantis project. Please take some time and come prepared with feedback based on your experience, what you would like to see changed, and suggestions for improvement. Every member of our team will have the chance to share their thoughts. I appreciate your taking the time to review this in advance and look forward to learning from your experiences.

Regards,
Saoirse

Structure Informal Conversations

An in-person meeting provides the space for people to hang out and get to know one another, but that's generally not the intended purpose. Often, we sit in meetings that have gone off track—ones in which we have a hard time reigning in side conversations. Even in small group settings, a few people always seem to be in a completely different conversation, which leads to a missed opportunity for productivity.

Try to give everyone five to seven minutes at the end of the meeting to hang out and catch up. Make sure this is something you formally write in your agenda, with "optional" next to it to give people the out if they need to run to another meeting. For example: *Informal catch-up (optional).* This works especially well if attendees don't get the chance to see each other often.

If your meeting starts off with an informal party and continues with sidebar conversations, it's going to be nearly impossible to get anything done. By structuring the time so attendees can socialize at the tail end of the meeting, you can say, "That sounds like such a fun trip, Kyle. Can't wait to chat about it more at our catch-up at the end!" Communicate to your attendees, "In an effort to stay on track and get everyone out of the meeting on time with follow-up items, we're going to add an optional, informal discussion for the last seven minutes. This means that we need to stay focused on the agenda for the rest of the meeting."

Ding! Time's Up

If your meetings tend to go off track, or certain people take over, use a timer to keep track and bring the team to order. Assign a leader to handle the timer and rotate the responsibility. "Team, each week someone will be in charge of making sure we stay focused and don't stray from our conversation. I want to make sure we're getting the most out of meetings and sticking to our agenda. We'll rotate this role monthly." This equalizes both the time individuals get to talk and the responsibility of keeping things on track.

You also can assign a specific amount of time for each agenda item, spending more time on the discussion and feedback section and less on the information sharing. This layout should be noted specifically on the agenda. For example: *Atlantis Project (discussion): 20 minutes.*

Get People Talking

I find that many people have amazing ideas to share, but they just don't feel that they are given the opportunity to share them. And sometimes, they might feel overshadowed by their peers. A great way to put someone at ease and build their confidence is by sharing how valuable they are to the conversation in your invitation.

Liz,

I would really value your input in our quarterly sales meeting this month. Attached you will find the agenda as well as our projected sales numbers. I think the group can really benefit from your expertise and experience making cold calls.

Regards,
Marlene

Once the meeting starts, the person who called the meeting is still responsible for encouraging participation. After all, you invited them for a reason. Here are some ways to get people talking:

Acknowledge participation. No matter what level of employee you are, it's always important to acknowledge that you heard and understood someone's contribution and to use clarifying questions when necessary. "That's a great point, Jan." "Thanks for bringing that up, Andrew." "Can you tell us more about that, Mark?" You don't have to be leading the meeting to show appreciation for someone else's input.

When you're face to face, you also have the unique advantage of using nonverbal cues to interact with your team—like smiling, nodding, or giving a sweet thumbs up. If you're virtual, take note of who has spoken and ask questions of those you haven't heard from.

Ask for feedback. If you're finding the conversation moving at a snail's pace try, "Can I get everyone's opinion on this?" "Does anyone have anything they would like to add?" Or try bringing similar viewpoints together and asking for additional input. "Piper and Na mentioned having difficulty getting in touch with their customer last week. Did anyone else have that issue?" It's OK to have a few moments of silence to let your team think over a question before you move on to the next thought. The important part is to let them know that you want to hear what they have to say.

Know your audience. It's important to know who you're in a meeting with and to adapt how you run it based on the personalities involved. At times, people may repeat the same information someone else said, whether it's just to hear themselves talk or because they didn't hear the other person cover it. In that situation, don't be snarky, and avoid phrases like "Jamie said that 10 minutes ago, weren't you listening?" Snark is never good for productive meeting vibes.

At other times, it may look like people are just staring at you and are not really paying attention. Try this: "Everyone, thanks for coming. I know it's been a busy week as we've been trying to hit our deadline. I promise as soon as we get through this content and discussion you can leave. I'm not going to keep you the whole hour." Read the room and act accordingly.

Small groups. Who said that we have to stay as a one large group for the whole meeting? I say break the rules and break up the group! Some parts of the meeting can be "pair share" where people work in pairs or small groups to discuss an idea and then later bring it back to the larger group. Here's a way to get someone to talk about what they discussed in a smaller group: "Brian, I overheard your thoughtful insights while you were working with Zach. Can you tell us a little more about your ideas on identifying a new target market? I think it will really benefit the group."

Some of the attendees might be more comfortable sharing with a peer than with the big group. Give them the space to do it.

HUMAN CONNECTION

Our company just launched a two-year leadership development program. To prepare for it, we brought together 35 employees from our locations both in and outside of the United States. The staff ranged from entry-level and hourly to our most sophisticated PhD roles. We divided them up into four diverse (generations, gender, race, positions) teams and asked them to use design thinking to create their ideal two-year leadership program. From there, we were able to take the best ideas from all four teams' concepts to create our leadership development program.

There were some topics, like conflict resolution, that would never have occurred to me to put on the list. But all four teams were adamant about it not only being included, but being offered as one of the first sessions. Although the program is still new, we've been receiving positive feedback from our employees about its relevancy to their roles and their willingness to recommend it to their colleagues. The program's success is, in large part, due to us taking the time to involve our diverse staff and to ask them what they need to be successful within our company. Also, at the beginning of the class, when I tell participants that the course was designed by peers who they admire, they immediately buy in and pay attention.

JAMIE LIBROT, Director of Talent Management and Global Strengths Leader

Gain insight into your behaviors and make adjustments. When you're the one taking over a meeting, you're probably not even aware. Start to take note of how often you're sharing your opinion and the non-verbal cues of your peers before they're about to speak. Do they move around in their chairs? Raise their hands? Start to stand up? When you know someone else is about to talk, hold onto your thoughts and give them a chance to share. Similarly, after you ask a question, take a few deep breaths before you either move on or provide insight. Don't jump in without giving people the time to process what you just said.

STRATEGIES TO INCREASE ENGAGEMENT IN MEETINGS

✔ Acknowledge participation.

✔ Ask for feedback.

✔ Know your audience.

✔ Form small groups.

✔ Gain insight into your behaviors and make adjustments.

HUMAN CONNECTION

Being self-aware is really important and one of my top strengths is communication. Several years ago, a trusted colleague of mine approached me and said, "Heather, you talk too much in meetings." I looked at her surprised and said, "I feel like I have all these great ideas that I want to share." She said, "You do, but you talk too much in our team meetings."

I think that feedback is a gift and I felt fortunate that my colleague cared enough about me to be honest. From then on, she sat across from me in meetings and we developed a signal. When I started to monopolize the conversation, she would casually move her hand above her head. This helped me to become more aware of how much I was actually speaking and stop as quickly as I could to give others an opportunity to speak.

I was then able to develop a strategy for navigating and leveraging my communication talent to ensure it was productive. Now, before I go to meetings, I give myself boundaries. I tell myself I can talk three times, so I better make them count, or that I cannot speak on a topic unless two other people have spoken to give them an opportunity to share. Although I've set these boundaries, I don't feel stifled. It's nice to hear my colleagues share their ideas, and I am no longer dominating the conversation.

HEATHER Z. KAY, Gallup Certified Strengths Coach

Be Smart About the "When"

Who loves a meeting first thing in the morning? Although I have not conducted an official survey, I would imagine it's pretty much no one. Perhaps not the most earth-shattering insight in this book, but someone out there needs to hear it: A 9:00 a.m. meeting on a Monday might not be the best idea.

I've worked for people who I'd wait until they had one cup—if not two—of coffee before I would ever think of asking an important question. Take stock of your attendees and when they are typically awake and ready to go. You also want to consider the time of year you're having the meeting. If this meeting spans various departments and it's during one department's busy season, acknowledge it. Don't ignore it! "I just wanted to say thank you to everyone for coming today and a special shout out to our sales team. I know this is an extremely hectic time of year for you as you're trying to make your year-end goals, and I appreciate your taking the time to attend. Your input on this project is extremely valuable."

If you don't say anything, people may think you're unaware of what's going on in the organization and the workload of others. To get a better pulse on the situation, send out a survey to your immediate team to identify the time of day that works best for everyone, or have an open conversation about what works best for all during your next gathering. Listen to your team's needs and make them feel heard.

Also consider alternate formats for meetings rather than the standard one-hour timeslot. Why not end when the content has been covered? Look at your agenda and gauge how long it will take to review. Try 15, 30, or even 45 minutes instead of defaulting to 60. (This is when that "set a timer" tip comes in handy!) If the meeting is scheduled for a full hour and you're finished in 50 minutes, let everyone go! If you don't drag the conversation longer than it has to be, you'll find that people are grateful to have been given10 extra minutes in their day.

Call Out the Elephant in the Room

There are going to be times when people just flat out don't want to be at your meeting. Sorry, it's the hard truth! People won't always be gung-ho on everything, no matter how important you think it is. Whether it's because they pulled the short straw or were delegated this project by their manager, you want to call out the elephant in the room. "I know that your plate is full right now, and you were asked last minute to fill in for John. I've had the same thing happen to me and it's frustrating. What questions can I answer to make the best use of your time?" Then just wait for them to respond. This brings to light the situation and puts that individual in the driver's seat to ask questions and steer the conversation. This approach can also help bring up issues that you didn't know existed and can be a great place from which to start building trust with this member of the organization.

Leave with a Takeaway

At the end of every meeting—yes, every single meeting—make a call to action. What did the group talk about, who is doing what, and who will follow up with whom and by when? Be clear on whether they're following up with one person, the whole group, or a cohort within the group. Without this, it feels like the meeting didn't need to happen in the first place. If you're in charge, make sure you're bringing all these pieces together, or delegate to someone to take notes and discuss follow-up.

If you've noticed that your manager is not making this happen, take on this role and have a conversation with your boss about the need for this closure. "Just to review what we talked about today: Jared, you're going to reach out to Grant about the TPS report and give our whole team an update next week at our meeting. John, you're going to talk to Stu about upgrading our teams' computers and send everyone in the room an email by Thursday on next steps. Did I miss anything?" Then get a verbal confirmation from the team before you leave the room. This is especially important for in-person meetings where people need to physically go out of their way to be there. You want everyone to know what they're responsible for and why they spent that last hour (or more) in a room—and not feel like they need a "I survived another meeting that could have been an email" sticker!

BE HUMAN. ACT HUMAN.

Taking time out of everyone's busy day for a meeting might not be your first choice of a well-spent afternoon. But if we're going to build authentic and meaningful relationships, and if we're going to build communication between colleagues and teams, meetings are important. (When done right!) If you're a person who likes to hear yourself talk and do not give others a chance to speak, stop! If you've been too nervous to voice an idea, take a deep breath and try. If you've never acknowledged a colleague's valuable contribution in a meeting, do it. Bring your in-person meetings to life so you're not dreading them, but rather, looking forward to insightful conversations with tangible takeaways.

CHAPTER 6

Connecting a Virtual Workforce

THE NINE-TO-FIVE, BUTT-IN-SEAT culture of traditional businesses is quickly going out the office (or living room, or coffee shop . . .) window. According to a 2018 study by Virgin Pulse and Future Workplace, remote work has increased by 115 percent over the past decade, with a third of global employees working remotely full time or very often.[1] As teams work across time zones and zip codes, it is more important than ever for them to learn to navigate, manage, and create a community among employees. Virtual teams are the present and future of work as companies look for employees based on talents, strengths, and experience, with less emphasis on their geographical location. However, even though this is the case, it doesn't mean we're prepared to deal with potential pitfalls in this environment.

When you don't physically see (or even have the chance to meet) the people you work with, it can be hard to set goals, spot disengaged team members, or even figure out how to work best together. I've spoken to many employees who've never even met their supervisor in person. This makes it even more difficult to develop relationships, get noticed, and bring people together. Whether you're a manager or an employee on a geographically diverse team, it's important to play an active role in creating an environment in which people have a connection with each other. It's not always easy, and it requires even more flexibility and a conscious effort on everyone's part to bridge the geographical divide.

Picture this: you're a remote employee of an organization. A small, central office employs about five people, and the rest of the company works virtually, like you. You have a fairly close relationship with your team lead and have been emailing back and forth about a client. The next day, you send an email and receive this reply:

Thank you for your email. I am out of the office on maternity leave until January.

If you need assistance before my return, please contact Avery Smith (avery@madeupemailaddress.com), or call 555-123-4567.

If this is a nonurgent matter I'll reply to your email upon my return.

You reread this email three times thinking that maybe you sent it to the wrong person, or you just don't yet have your normal amount of caffeine in your system. You've just found out via the "out of office" message that the same person who you've been working with for the past few years—and closely on this project—was not only expecting, but just had their baby. On top of that, you should be reaching out to someone you don't know in their absence.

On the surface, this email looks pleasant, provides necessary information for immediate contact, and gives a timeframe for return. But, for the people who weren't in the small office having daily face-to-face interactions, this "announcement" came as quite a shock. This is a true story from someone I interviewed for this book. The team lead had a planned maternity leave over the course of several months, but somehow, she didn't let her virtual team of 30 employees know. Now, there are things that come up suddenly, and there are things that are very personal and not necessary to share. But, for everything else, it's important to give a heads-up to the people you don't see on a daily basis. Needless to say, the employee whose story I'm sharing was left feeling like they weren't part of the team. They felt unappreciated and completely disconnected from others in the organization.

Technology can be amazing. We have the power to be in a million places at once, connect with people from all over the globe, and save our company and ourselves thousands of dollars in time and travel with just the click of a button. But what does this mean for building authentic relationships with other members of the organization?

The convenience of working from home in our pajamas or from a coffee shop down the street means that we need to be more intentional in creating a virtual environment where people feel heard, valued, and appreciated. We don't want them to feel like they're on a deserted island and the last one to find out about a crucial event or change. Everyone, regardless of level, can play a part in creating these spaces and enhancing their team's culture.

First Impressions

If you're taking on a new role as manager or project lead, or you hired someone new for your team, it's a good idea to schedule an initial "get to know you" video meeting. If you're the newly hired employee, ask your supervisor and fellow team members for one-on-one meetings. These introductory video meetings give you a chance to get to know the people who work with and for you and can help you establish rapport early on.

HUMAN CONNECTION

When I first started to work from home, I initiated video calls with my boss every two weeks. We discussed how things were going both on my side and theirs to ensure the transition went smoothly and I was still meeting their expectations. My supervisor and I continue to have open discussions about my long-term goals because I don't want anything to be a surprise during my formal review. We both know that it's a two-way street and want to make sure that my lack of physical presence in the office is not an excuse to not take on more challenging work or continue to be a leader (which are generally the two things needed to be considered for a promotion). I also have chosen to travel to the main office for department-wide meetings and training sessions to get both face time with my supervisor and to reconnect with my colleagues. I have found that to not get lost in the virtual workspace, you have to make an active effort to communicate with your supervisor and to keep them updated on your goals and progress of assignments. Taking the time and making the extra effort to travel to our main office also helps me show that I am serious about my role and making a difference within the company.

TAYLOR D., Certified Public Accountant

Give Them a Toolbox

One of the first steps to building a virtual team is to select the appropriate tools. If we're not using the most effective equipment, software, or platforms, we're not giving ourselves the chance to build meaningful relationships. But before we throw money at the latest tech trend, we need to establish what our organization and teams are looking to accomplish (now and in the future), what types of interactions would help make this happen, and what other functions would be helpful for increasing efficiency and productivity.

I won't be listing the specific technologies by name, as this environment is constantly changing, but there are some specific functions you should consider when you're choosing the appropriate communication tools for your organization. You'll almost always need to be able to

- Access and work collaboratively on graphics and documents in real time.
- Communicate with your team through web, video, and audio conferencing.
- Find and schedule common meeting times.
- Interact through a social network.

- Manage projects and workflow through scheduling and task assignments.

- Share and store files and documents through a central secured portal.

Host a Technology Training

After you or your organization has chosen the platform(s) you'll be using, it's essential for the team to understand how and when to use it. Whether you're the one in the driver's seat or you bring in an expert, host a training that walks everyone through the platform's key functions. Demonstrate where to click to search and share documents, how to start and end a video meeting, and any other areas that are key to your team's success. Share the best practices and rules for using message boards with clear direction of their purpose, "This board is for sharing updates and for questions pertaining to technology roll-outs in the finance department." Being as clear as possible about not only how to use the technology, but when and why, is important.

Give your employees an opportunity to test out the platform and provide a contact for any questions that should arise after the session so employees don't feel stranded when they can't access information. This may seem like common sense, but to maximize its usage, it's important to have everybody on the same page with this technology from day one.

Establish Communication Protocols

Organizations often stop technology training once people know how to use it, and they don't take time to establish best practices for use. In order to have effective communication in geographically dispersed teams, employees need to know what buttons to push and—most importantly—when. Having an open conversation with the group to identify which technology should be used for which circumstances can save a lot of frustration and create opportunities to enhance productivity and build relationships. These conversations should address which platform is best for

- Sharing and sending information
- Reviewing information
- Providing updates
- Asking in-depth questions
- Providing quick answers
- Sharing new information
- Sending cat videos

Even more important than training teams on how to use the technology is establishing team norms for people in varying locations in order to provide all employees with a reference point they can use to hold themselves and others accountable. Whether or not you're in a leadership role, you can bring up these areas for discussion:

Work hours. Because people are working across all time zones, discuss what hours the team needs to be online and available. Is it nine to five in their time zone, the central office's zone, or are other hours more productive? Once this is established, have all employees share their schedules with all members of the team through their email signatures, "out of office" messages, and your internal instant messaging system.

How to be seen. How should employees show they are available for messaging, meetings, or other communication? Should they use the color indications in the messaging platform (green, yellow, or red), block off time on their calendars, a combination of both, or is there another method preferred?

Check-ins. It's easy to get sucked in to your work and not always check in with your team or supervisor about your progress. This can cause frustration for your boss, who may not know what you're working on, or for your coworkers, if they're waiting for you to complete a step. Many organizations and project managers have created "deliverable dashboards" to track progress and keep everyone in the loop. These can be something as simple as a shared spreadsheet or something more specific to your organization. You can also host one-on-one check-ins, but make sure you're clear on their frequency (weekly, monthly, or even daily). This is not about babysitting, and it's not just about tracking progress on a project. It's also about maintaining a strong relationship between employees and coworkers.

HUMAN CONNECTION

Communication is the key to everything. It's important to make sure my staff knows that I'm hearing them and that they're hearing me. It's a two-way street. Every Friday, I have one-on-one meetings with my team leads who report directly to me. For my virtual team members at our North Carolina office, we use Skype and sometimes phone. The team leads go over their own workload and if there are any issues with any of their staff. As a group, the team leads and I meet biweekly to go over various initiatives and goals we have for the month and goals we have for the year. We check in with work goals and to see how things are going. I also have a monthly meeting with the entire staff (admins, coordinators, proposal development leads, and team leads). In addition to that, we have a quarterly business development (inside and outside sales team) meeting. I present on the internal pieces, including our key performance indicators (KPIs); the director of business development presents all of the financial information and KPIs for their team. I also go visit other offices once a quarter, virtual employees come to our main office for various workshops, and we have a yearly, in-person conference for our whole team. We physically see each other about three to four times a year. Everybody is informed on everything and this is something I strongly believe in. I report directly to our company's vice president, who also believes in transparent and open communication. It's the foundation in our department.

KAREN SWANSON, Proposal Development Group Manager,
Business Development (US) at Almac Clinical Services

Team meetings. Will the team be doing virtual meetings once a week, or at another interval? Or do only certain members have to attend certain functions? Who should a person contact if they can't make a meeting due to an extenuating circumstance? Make sure everyone is clear on who needs to be where and when, and you'll avoid missed connections and any *"Wait, what meeting?"* confusion. Creating a manual of these guidelines makes them more official, allows people to reference them in the future, and makes it easier for new employees to understand the virtual workforce expectations.

Speaking of meetings, that's another place where you'll want to create team norms. Although working virtually may be old hat for some, other employees might be new to this type of work. More distractions and nuances can crop up for meetings in which people are not in the same location. Here are some suggestions for virtual team meeting guidelines:

- Find a place that's free of background noise and outside distractions. (Put your dog outside and maybe let the kids watch YouTube in another room.)
- Use headphones.
- Turn on your unavailable status.
- Turn off sound notifications.
- Avoid distractions. Act like you're in the room with everyone else and put away your phone, turn off your TV, and don't work on another project.
- Speak clearly (and remember to turn off your mute button before speaking).
- Use visual aids, if possible.

If you're on video, look into the camera as much as possible when speaking and listening.

If you're finding yourself zoning out during virtual meetings, try these hacks:

- Put a sticky note or photo under the camera so you remember to focus there.

- Close all other windows on your computer.

- Remove all other devices from your desk.

- Physically stand up when you're speaking.

You also want to consider the timing of meetings, especially if you're working across time zones. Try having your weekly meetings at the same time for one quarter, then rotating them to a different time for the next. You want to ensure that employees in one time zone aren't stuck always waking up early or staying up late to catch a meeting during nine-to-five hours in another part of the world.

Create Opportunities for More Engagement

With web conferencing, discussion, and messaging boards, we have so many options for starting and continuing conversations. The key is to find new and innovative ways to keep people engaged. When conducting meetings, try

Setting up breakout rooms. These virtual rooms allow for small group discussion within the larger meeting. The groups can meet for a period of time to discuss a topic and then report back to the larger group.

Allowing people to share their screen. When someone is sharing information, allow them to display their screen so everyone can follow along. This gives them ownership of material while allowing people to further understand what they're sharing.

Creating a virtual note-taking space. Designate someone to take notes during the meeting and have them visible. Without nonverbal cues and with the potential for technology glitches, you want to make sure everyone is hearing the same information so they can ask questions and chime in with ideas in real time.

HUMAN CONNECTION

To increase participation on web conferencing platforms, I've kicked off sessions with a poll. This immediately captures engagement and then you can reflect on responses during the meeting. It helps people stay engaged and included in the guided discussion.

You can also use these platforms to mimic real life. Discussion boards are a great way to engage on specific topics and often lead to spin off conversations. Using the "@" functionality to call on a person or a group of people who may have more knowledge or experience can help connect them in ways they are already using (e.g., Facebook, Instagram, Twitter). These relationships may start virtually and lead to direct person-to-person connections.

KRISTEN TOPPING, SHRM-SCP

Talk Beyond Business

Schedules can get crazy and workloads pile up, leaving days, weeks, and even months between conversations with coworkers not in the same office space. Finding opportunities to get your whole team together may be difficult, whereas finding spaces for smaller group conversations may be more feasible. This works not just for work-specific conversations, but also for more teambuilding and "get to know you" sessions. Invite a colleague for an informal video call or create a shared sign-up document for people to opt-in for an online chat. You can also provide topics for discussion to give everyone a starting point. Establishing a social relationship with coworkers—even when it's not in person—will help you feel more connected to the organization and less like you're on a deserted island.

Think about starting or being involved in a virtual social activity:

Fitness challenge	Sync your wearables to see who gets the most steps in a week.
Book club	Every month, have a new person choose a book and then gather online to talk about it.
Virtual happy hour	Grab a glass of wine, beer, or sparkling water and chat away with your coworkers.
Virtual lunches	Order delivery or have your team members expense a take-out meal to enjoy together.

Try to Meet In-Person

In a virtual world where there is so much clutter, it's easy to get distracted. We can easily text and get in a doodle or two all while "paying attention" from behind a screen. And, of course, virtual conversations can still have barriers. Being able to see nonverbal cues is important. Finding an opportunity to be physically in the same place is crucial, whether it happens once a year at the company retreat, when it's all-hands-on-deck during the busy season, or on a more frequent basis. No matter how hard we try, nothing can replace that in-person, human connection. Although not every company or person can always meet in person due to distance and cost, here are some ideas to make it a little easier:

- If there's a central office where a few people you work with are stationed, ask for permission to travel once a quarter to have an in-person meeting.

- Attend a professional development workshop, conference, training, or seminar close to corporate headquarters and work a day from that office.

- Host an in-person team retreat at a neutral location so all members can meet one another.

- Schedule your annual or quarterly review sessions in a central location or travel to your employees' headquarters.

- If you're traveling and will be close to where one of your teammates or employees lives, ask to grab lunch.

By making yourself available in person, you can get a real-time pulse on engagement and satisfaction. It's hard to see how people interact with each other in a virtual space, but in person, you can see who sits with whom, who seems disengaged, who is staring in space, and where the action is happening. Are people hanging out in the break room and saying hi to each other when they pass in the halls? Or is everyone's door shut, and theirs heads are down, focused on their computers? These are things you won't find on any fancy platform. And as an employee, spending in-person time with your boss can ensure they don't forget about you! Getting some quality face time with your supervisor can help you get a better gauge on your performance, areas for improvement, and future with the company.

You Are Your Word

Do what you say you're going to do! Maybe this goes without saying, but your word is important, especially on a virtual team. It's essential to follow through on your commitments, be on time to meetings, and keep others in the loop on what you're working on. Unlike working in an office, you can't stop a coworker in the hallway or pull them aside while they're heating up their lunch to check on the status of a project. Don't leave other people hanging or wondering if you'll ever get back to them. Honor your word and be communicative.

Biannual Check-Ups

Establishing a twice-a-year check-up can help you gauge how your team communicates. Just like being proactive with your health by going to the doctor for your yearly physical, these check-ups will give you the chance to improve the "health" of your virtual team. Without setting aside time to specifically talk about strategies, best practices, and potential breakdowns, you might be missing key opportunities to enhance relationships and connections among your team. A check-up can be as simple as a 60-minute meeting that follows a survey on the following information:

- Most commonly used medium to share information (email, call, face-to-face virtual meeting)

- Frequency of information sharing (five times a day, once a week, etc.)

- Length of information sharing sessions (30 minutes, one hour)

- Attitude toward existing communication tools

- Suggestions for enhancement of sharing tools

The biannual meeting would not only be a review of the results your team gathered, but it would also be an open forum for providing suggestions on new technology, establishing new practices, and airing any virtual communication concerns or issues that have not been previously addressed.

BE HUMAN. ACT HUMAN.

Working with people from across the globe can be difficult, and sometimes even feel a bit . . . unhuman. But it's the reality of our future workplace, so we need to work on making it, well, a little more human. It takes extra effort to establish rapport, build relationships, and improve communication when we're not seeing our colleagues in person. If we don't make an active effort to get to know the people who work with us, we'll quickly feel isolated and disengaged. We all have a voice and an opportunity to create the culture we want for our virtual teams, so embrace new ways to connect via technology and with a little creativity.

PART III

Change Is the
Only Constant

CHAPTER 7

Breaking Through the Screen Barrier

SO MUCH HAS CHANGED and will continue to change with technology. But right now, email remains a major form of communication in our work culture. Email gives everyone the opportunity to reach each other regardless of location, whether they're in Baltimore or Brazil, and it provides a means for correspondence. It is the universal language of business correspondence across the world.

Because of its ubiquity, it's easy to just hit "send" on an email without taking the time to build a personal connection with the recipient. We often use email to disseminate information or get updates and leave our personalities out of the conversation. Sometimes it's hard to remember that there's an actual human on the other side of that recipient name—especially when they won't answer.

But our email doesn't just have to be a forum for the old, "Just checking in to see if you received my last message . . . ." You can also use email to get to know colleagues who you might not see that often. You can use it as an opportunity to add something personal and let a coworker know that you care. "Rachel, congratulations on your baby girl! I just got the company-wide announcement and she's adorable. How are you feeling?" With just a few tweaks and a bit of care, we can enhance our professional relationships through email.

Toxic Tones

"Sarah, as I've previously mentioned, stop sending me cat videos."

"Garrett, just wondering: Did you take my lunch from the fridge?"

"Kyle, not sure if you saw my last email or the one before that, or the one I sent you before that one. Actually, do you ever check your email?"

We've all done it. You know the snarky attitude that comes across in your emails where you're annoyed that the person on the other end isn't responding or just isn't paying attention. But, being passive-aggressive can quickly destroy relationships. Here are some of the worst phrases you can write if someone hasn't responded to your last email:

- "Not sure if you saw my last email"
- "Any update on this?"
- "Sorry for the double email"
- "Re-attaching for convenience"
- "Sorry to bother you, but . . ."
- "Just wondering"
- "I'm not sure if my email ever made it to you as I haven't heard back"
- "It appears you forgot to . . ."

And here are some pretty bad ones when you think the other person should already know the answer to the questions they're asking:

- "Per our last email" (The mother of all email snark!)
- "Per our conversation"
- "As discussed"
- "As previously stated"

- "First of all"

- "In case you missed it"

- "According to my records"

- "Please note"

But why are they bad, and why should we stop using them? Because these phrases can often come across as accusatory, and you can almost see your mom waving her finger back and forth as you read them. They set a poor tone for the email and can immediately turn off your recipient. They are also unnecessary add-ons that serve no positive value. Instead of using these phrases, you can either copy and paste a previous response or reframe or paraphrase your previous answer and leave the "per my previous email" out of the equation.

Emotion can be hard to get across in an email, but the follow-up phrases just listed can leave your colleagues feeling frustrated and unmotivated to respond. And yes, of course intentionally not answering an email and letting it sit in their inbox is also passive aggressive. But don't be the one to set that tone. Even phrases like "sorry to bother you" or "re-attaching for your convenience," which are intended to sound polite, usually have an underlying (and commonly understood) meaning. Translation: "I need an answer." So instead of beating around the bush in a "nice" way, come out and ask the question directly.

To figure out how to replace these faux-pas phrases, first determine whether you want your recipient to provide you with additional information or if you just need to know that they received your email. This determines what your follow-up phrasing should be. If you're frustrated and know that you're going to sink into old habits: write out your email, save it, and then come back later and update it after you've had a minute to cool down. Never email when you're angry! Here are some easy phrases to swap in for those passive aggressive no-no's:

LOOKING FOR INFORMATION AND FOLLOW UP	NO ACTION REQUIRED, CONFIRMATION REQUEST
▪ "(Name), I have some new information I wanted to share with you that may impact your feedback on my previous email." Give an update and share new information, then reference the previous request.	▪ "I wanted to check in to see if you had any questions regarding . . ."
▪ "If I don't hear from you by (date), I'm going to move forward."	▪ "I wanted to follow up with you to see if you received my previous email about (x) and if you had any questions."
▪ "Hi (name), can you please let me know where you stand on (x). I need to follow up with (person) by (date) and value your input."	▪ "Hi (name), do you have any questions regarding (x)?"
▪ "Hi, (name), I just wanted to see if you had input on (x). I value your opinion and would like to include it in my communication with (person)."	▪ "(Name), this is just a reminder about (x). Please do not hesitate to reach out if you have any questions."
Subject Lines: "Response Needed," "Timely"	

People will appreciate that you're being honest and direct—you're getting to the root of what you need without all that surface language.

Why Am I CC'd on This?

We receive so many emails each day that it's easy for things to get lost. And by so many, I mean we receive 269 billion consumer and business emails each day, and this is expected to rise to 319.6 billion in the next few years.[1] The more we can do to cut down on the clutter, the better! This includes not adding to it. I know, sometimes sending an email is just easier. You have something on your mind and you want someone to know about it, you need to send a file, or you're using it as a written record.

One of the first conversations I have with my clients or teammates is about how we can effectively communicate through email. This wasn't something I did until I noticed that certain pieces of information would become buried in email chains, that some people preferred to communicate in person, or that we needed a consistent method for sending updates on the status of projects. Having these conversations now helps me set group norms and expectations. Here are the questions I'm sure to cover:

- "When we send emails, do you prefer them to be separated by subject so you can track it that way? Or do you prefer fewer, longer emails that cover a variety of topics?"

- "What should we cover via email versus face to face or by other means?"

- "Are there certain types of emails you want to be cc'd on?"

- "What is the best way to let you know the results of a project I am working on?"

- "What is the expected response time for emails, both internally and to our external partners and clients?"

- "If an internal email is not answered within our designated time period, how should we update the subject to indicate a follow-up request? Would writing '2nd request: subject' be appropriate?"

- "How many back-and-forth email exchanges on the same topic are acceptable before we make the conversation face to face?"

If an email conversation has been going back and forth for a while, it's easy to lose sight of its original intent; especially when you add on another recipient after the initial email. No one wants to scroll through the entire conversation to figure out what's meant for them in the bread crumbs of information "found below."

Instead of just adding a cc or forwarding a thread, try creating a new thread and then copy and paste the vital information from the old thread to the new one to get everyone on the same page. This extra step of boiling things down to what your current recipients need to know really shows that you value their time so they're not sifting through random content that doesn't make sense or apply to them. You can make things even simpler by summarizing using bullets instead of paragraphs. Getting straight to the point and without all the fluff makes your email easier to read, digest, and understand for your recipients. This way, you're not the reason someone is staring at their inbox saying, "Why am I even on this email?"

Read and Respond

Reflect on the group communication norms your team came up with at the beginning of the project and stick with them. If your group decided that answering emails within 24 to 48 hours was important, then make a habit of following through in that time period. We all get it—things happen—but make it a point to always follow up. If you don't have the answers, are waiting for something, or are not ready to make a full response, just send a quick email update. "Thanks for the information, Kim. I am waiting to hear back from purchasing about your question and will update you as soon as I have the most recent information." "Thank you for your email. I will review this and get back to you by tomorrow afternoon." You can also send a simple, "Received." or "Got it." depending on your relationship with the recipient. Don't force people to have to reach back out to you for an answer. You don't want to develop a reputation as someone who is not responsive.

And if you encourage follow-ups when you're on the receiving end, let people know. One of my colleagues put out a clever disclaimer during a team meeting, "If I don't get back to you within 48 hours, I may have lost your email. Please email me again to make sure I get back to you." We all knew that if we didn't hear back from them in two days, it was time to follow up.

Think Before You Send

I'll be the first to admit that I've preemptively sent an email. I breezed through it, thought that everything was good to go, hit send, and then bam . . . *add* was spelled *ass*. A quick run to my supervisor cleared the air, but my heart was pounding from the minute I noticed the error. I've also gotten recall requests from colleagues who've realized that they sent something that wasn't work appropriate. By that time, we had already gotten it, read it, and then reread it to see what the cause of such a fuss was. Just remember, before you hit send, make sure you're sending it to the right person/people, that it has the attachments you note in your message, that it is free of any spelling or grammatical errors, and that it is work appropriate. Try using the following checklist to keep on track.

EMAIL CHECKLIST

✔ Check for spelling and grammatical errors.

✔ Make sure "To," "CC," and "BCC" lines are accurate.

✔ Does the subject line appropriately reflect the email content?

✔ If noted, confirm attachments referenced are included.

✔ Confirm the content is clear, straightforward, and easy to read.

✔ Make sure appropriate contact information is included.

HUMAN CONNECTION

One of the biggest email communication errors I have observed over the years is not checking on who is on the distribution list. I can remember one case in particular when a vice president at AT&T asked her team for 360-degree feedback. One of her direct reports, a person she brought with her from a previous position she held, and a close friend, decided to provide her with some supportive, yet judgmental, feedback.

It would have been well received had he shared it with just her. However, he didn't check the distribution list and it went out to everyone on her team. It was not completely complimentary, so there were very hard feelings and a lot of anger. It took some time before their relationship returned to its original level. This all could have been avoided had he checked who the email was actually being sent to.

LORI ROSENTHAL, Strategic Human Resources Partner

Set Email Expectations

We talk a lot about work/life balance and work/life integration, but we don't necessarily set the expectations around what that means in terms of electronic communication. As a supervisor, if you say that people don't have to answer their email on off hours, but then you send emails during that time, give your team the heads up that they don't have to respond. Or just flat out don't send emails during off hours. We have to practice what we preach.

For the benefit of the team you work with, make sure everyone understands your off-hour email tendencies and expectations. The best way to make sure everyone is on the same page is to have a conversation about it. "Team, I know I send you emails on nights and weekends. I am going to try to do a better job of waiting until normal business hours to send them because I know many of you take the time to answer them during your off hours, and that is not my expectation. I want you to enjoy your time with your family and friends and not worry about what is sitting in your inbox." Or, "I tend to send emails during off hours, but I do not have the expectation that you will respond. When something comes up, I want to pass it along as soon as I can so I do not leave you out of the loop."

If you're not a supervisor and feel inundated with emails during off hours, speak to your manager about it. "Paula, I wanted to touch base about your expectations in terms of response time to emails. My goal is to get back to people within 24 hours, but sometimes you send emails on nights and weekends. Is your intention for me to answer them during that time, or is the next business day appropriate?" Or, "I notice that I get a lot of emails after the office closes and I don't have work email set up on my personal phone. Is there an expectation that I do so?" However, keep in mind that such conversations should be had with a team as a whole so everyone is on the same page, not just the two people originally involved.

At times, information may need to be addressed during off hours. This could be for last-minute client changes, a closing deadline, or in an emergency situation. It's important to establish a policy where the manager or project lead provides a heads-up to employees to ensure they meet their expectations. This can be done in person, too. "Jane, I know you're headed out for the weekend in a few hours, but I still haven't heard from our client about the T-shirt orders. We need to get the order in before Saturday at noon for it to ship on Tuesday. They should be emailing me within the next few hours. I'll forward you their request as soon as I have it for you to push the order through. Thanks for handling this on such short notice."

It's Not That Serious

Stop using the "high importance" feature if you don't need to! I get it, everything we say and do is important, but if it's not actually urgent, you're going to turn people off and quickly lose the opportunity to build a strong working relationship. You know the story of the boy who cried wolf and when the wolf finally came, nobody cared, right? Same thing. When you actually need something, people won't pay attention if you're constantly putting everything on high alert. Here are some things to think about before you hit that red exclamation point:

- Is the deadline within the next 24–48 hours?

- Did a meeting scheduled for the same day get cancelled? Is there a last-minute meeting that they need to attend?

- Does this need to be a top priority because this response affects the work/process timeline of others?

- Is there an actual emergency? (If it's this one, go beyond the email and make a call or talk to someone in person!)

- Is there cake in the breakroom? (OK, not really high importance–worthy, but save a piece for me!)

Think about if it's time-sensitive or if there's an important piece of information that needs to be added to an agenda on an upcoming meeting. If you honestly answered "yes" to one or more of these questions, it's

OK to send your email with high importance. If none of these apply, and you just want people to know something that you feel is important— avoid unnecessary use of the button. You don't want to dilute the actual importance of a future email.

Change Up Your Signoff

One of the things I've struggled with for years is how to end an email. I used "Best" as the tried and true for years, but it just never seemed to give a personal touch. It always felt a little blah. Writing something with a little flair can add an extra impression and give people a little more of your personality. It can also lead to a higher response rate!

Here are some closings to spice up your emails. Go with the ones that speak to your personality, to the nature of your email, and to the intended recipient. You can also rotate your closing phrase, so people don't get the impression it's just a generic signoff or part of a signature.

TONE	SIGN-OFF
Neutral	▪ Cheers ▪ Take Care ▪ Warmly ▪ Best
Appreciative	▪ Many Thanks ▪ Thank You ▪ Warm Regards ▪ Warmest Regards
Formal, but not stiff	▪ Regards ▪ Kind Regards ▪ Best Regards

Add a Headshot

An easy way to personalize your email is by adding a headshot to your signature. In one of my previous roles, our organization made the conscious decision to change the email templates to accommodate a photo for a more personalized feel. The organization held free headshot sessions, emailed us our photos, and instructed us on how to add it to our email signature and to other digital platforms.

My organization realized that signatures with just names, titles, and contact information didn't add much context to the person behind the message. Having seen a photo also helps if you're meeting someone for the first time and you can connect the name from their email to the face that you're seeing. And it doesn't even have to be a formal headshot. Something from the shoulders up, smiling, and taken within the last decade will do the trick.

A strong signature that informs a reader of the best and most convenient ways to contact you should include

- Name
- Title
- Organization
- Contact information (phone/email)
- Professional social channels (if applicable)
- Video or other timely content

Confused? Just Ask

Let's say an email you receive doesn't have all the information you're looking for, or you're having trouble following an email that seems to be going in a million different directions. You're now in a position in which you either have to ask some questions to clarify the main points or spend some time raking through the clutter. Your response email can set the tone for future conversations. Paraphrase and then ask a direct question about your responsibilities: "I want to make sure I am understanding your question correctly and providing you with accurate information. Would you like me to find the data for calls made in March of 2019 and compare that data to numbers from the previous year?"

If possible, an in-person or over-the-phone conversation may be best. This helps avoid overloading email boxes and can keep the email conversation on track.

Add Something Personal

An easy way to not only share information but also to show that you care is by asking a question about someone's personal life—something that they shared with you and you want to follow up on. This doesn't have to be in a separate email. Include a personal touch to a work-related email with a simple, "I heard you adopted a dog, how is that going? Do you have any pictures?" "Congratulations on the promotion. I know you've been working hard, and I'm really excited for you!" "Last time we talked you weren't feeling well, are you feeling any better?" Use the information that you have and ask a question to check in to see how they are doing. Just make sure it's just the two of you on the email thread. A little human connection via email can go a long way. It shows you were listening, care, and are interested in what is going on in the other person's life.

BE HUMAN. ACT HUMAN.

Even though you can't physically see a person, it doesn't mean they don't exist. Another *real person* is always on the other side of that "send" button. If someone isn't answering your emails in a timely matter, assume the best intentions and follow up. Nothing good ever comes from being passive aggressive. By writing a small (but thoughtful) question, or by adding a photo in your signature, you can take your email to the next level and bring a human element to something that doesn't always feel so personal.

CHAPTER 8

Communicating with Intention—
Choosing a Medium

WITH SO MANY WAYS to interact, it can be confusing to figure out which medium will work best in each situation. Without taking a step back to identify the most effective form of delivery, your message has the real possibility of not only getting lost, but also being completely forgotten. Marshall McLuhan, in his book, *Understanding Media: Extensions of Man,* said it perfectly, "The medium *is* the message."[1] Although there's no rule book on this, you should consider a few things to get the most out of your interactions.

Let's start with who you're trying to communicate with. If it's your supervisor, try deferring to their preferred method. This will likely result in a shorter response time and a higher level of engagement than if you use a method they're not as in-tune with. Start by asking, "How do you like to be communicated with?" or "What is the best way to get in touch with you?" This gives them the authority to choose and it gives you the inside track on their preference.

Don't assume everybody prefers the same method. It's best to be direct and ask, letting the individual in authority know you're considering the most effective communication so you can get the job done efficiently. But what if you're trying to communicate with someone at the same level as you, or the person of authority does not give you a specific answer?

Here are some guidelines to help you navigate that decision. And just so we're on the same page, you don't have to hit on all of these points every single time you send an email. But depending on the scenario, these are some things to consider before you hit send.

Email

Here are times when email is likely the way to go:

Straightforward information. You're sending out something that requires no conversation or questions and is limited to upfront content (invitation, calendar of upcoming events, etc.).

Different time zones. We're often working with people all over the globe and it can be hard to sync up times for a call or video chat. Email can work well if you're trying to relay information to someone outside your time zone. If the information falls into a "more complex" bucket, use email to schedule a conversation to ensure you're both available at the same time.

Off hours. If you're working late and need to get information out, email is much better than a phone call that interrupts family dinner. Consider the emotions of who you are reaching out to outside of work hours. Most people want a break from their jobs, and email is the least invasive of the communication means. Remember that most things you need to discuss are not emergencies, and sending a late-night email ensures the information is in their inbox first thing in the morning.

When the recipient can be chatty. If there is someone who tends to hold you up when you're just relaying information, email can be a nice way to keep things on task. They still get the information they need, and you don't have to be on the phone with them for an hour about unrelated topics.

CYA (nicer way of saying "covering your ass"). There are times when you just need information in writing. You can always have a face-to-face conversation and then summarize it and send it via email. But if you're looking for documentation, email is the way to go. Try being more specific by mentioning documented approvals, recorded history of longer-running conversations, and other details that will be good to have on record.

Follow up. If you have a terrible memory or you have a history of taking bad notes, email can be a way to recap a conversation to make sure you're on the same page.

USES FOR EMAIL

✔ Providing straightforward information

✔ Distributing content during off hours and with colleagues in different time zones

✔ Documenting and following up with information

Phone, Video Chat, or In-Person

For anything deeper than what works in email, having an in-person conversation is usually the best way to communicate. This gives us the chance to see body language and hear the other person's tone. But in today's working environment, that's not always possible. With the constant improvement in audio and video technology, video or phone conversations can have a similar impact to in-person conversations (at least until my dream of teleportation is available). Consider the following scenarios for times when a more audio/visual experience would result in more effective communication.

High emotions. Whenever there is the potential for something to be emotional, you want to talk to the other party in person. Messages can easily get confused through email, and when you're having a conversation either face to face or over the phone, the tone is much easier to navigate. We tend to overreact when we don't understand the full context. Whether it's apologizing for a mistake, clarifying a miscommunication, or explaining some tough feelings about a project gone awry—a face-to-face or voice-to-voice conversation is needed.

HUMAN CONNECTION

Too often, we allow our own feelings of inadequacy to decode the messages we receive from others. When we cannot read their body language (are they smiling, relaxed, angry, crying, etc.) or hear the tone in their voice (upbeat, depressed, loud, etc.), we fill in what we are feeling at the time. Bold text, italics, fonts, punctuation—all alter our meanings. We need to take the time to understand what is being said, compare it with the person we know, and reach out when they don't match.

LORI ROSENTHAL, Strategic Human Resources Partner

Urgent issues. If you need information immediately from someone and their office is two doors down, get up and go talk with them. If they're not in your physical location, but it's during office hours, give them a call or start a video chat. When you send an email, you're not guaranteed to get an immediate response to an urgent issue (even after adding one of those red flags). By flagging them down a bit more literally, you're more likely to start moving toward a solution.

Feedback. Providing feedback should always be done verbally, especially when you're providing constructive feedback. This allows the other person the opportunity to ask questions, gain insight, and ask for support right away without anything getting lost in email translation. This does not apply to official reviews that need to be documented, and always paired with conversations, but are written out for logistics and support.

The endless email circle. We all get involved in emails that start innocently, but drag on, leave questions unanswered, or even start a whole new thread of topics. The email chain that never ends is frustrating. It can be much more efficient to have a fluid conversation with someone then it is to sift through days of emails to search for info and answers. If you know the conversation is going to require a lot of questions, you'll save time, energy, and headaches by stopping in someone's office or picking up the phone. Always consider if others need to be included in this conversation as well to make sure they can join in the fun.

USES FOR PHONE, VIDEO CHAT, OR IN-PERSON CONVERSATION

✔ Supporting dialogue with high emotional impact

✔ Discussing urgent issues

✔ Providing feedback

✔ Ending the endless email circle

Text and Instant Messaging

Although email, face to face, and phone calls may be some of the more common ways to communicate in the workplace, the use of texting and messaging platforms is on the rise, especially for Millennials and Gen Z. However, these insta-methods can tricky. More so than other mediums, they are dependent on company culture, individual preference, and the relationships between recipients.

If your organization doesn't provide a company phone, texting someone's personal number might be off limits, and doing so might be a seen as inappropriate, regardless of intent. Even if you do have a manager or coworker's number, it's important to ask for permission before you text something work related so you do not cross any lines. Texting isn't the best form of communication in which to do business and it should be reserved for personal conversations.

Some organizations have an instant messaging (IM) system; however, this isn't intended for lengthy back-and-forth exchanges in which people feel chained to their desk, waiting for your next message or response. You also want to keep an eye out for availability settings so you do not disturb someone while they are in a meeting or working on a time-sensitive project. Before using either of these mediums, consider the following scenarios:

Casual content. If you're leaving for lunch, left brownies in the kitchen, or need access to a shared document, an instant message is perfect. Once you've asked your question or shared your brief information, it's time to move on and get down to business. Don't take this interaction for a full-on conversation.

Conversation primer. Instead of heading straight for someone's office, use instant messaging to both save you extra steps and gauge if someone is available for a quick chat. "Are you free? Can I pop in your office and ask you a question?" "Can I give you a call in five minutes to review the Anderson case?"

Quick answer. Most questions are quick in delivery, but the answers can be lengthy. When choosing either of these mediums, first decide whether the answer is straightforward. If so, a simple message or text can be the way to go. When you're sending long-winded tasks through IM, however, most likely you're leaving the person on the other end frantically copying and pasting instructions into a document before they accidentally close the messaging window and the instructions all go away. An IM also suggests a sense of urgency for that person to stop what they're doing and complete your request. If it's complex or a full-on project, leave the IM out of it. If your exchange goes back and forth three times with no resolution, it's time to hop on a call or have a face-to-face conversation.

USES FOR TEXT AND INSTANT MESSAGING

✔ Sharing casual information

✔ Priming an in-person, virtual, or phone conversation

✔ Disseminating information with straightforward and quick answers

BE HUMAN. ACT HUMAN.

Whether emailing, texting, calling, or popping in to a colleague's office, stay in tune with how the recipient is receiving your communication and if it is working for them. Not good at picking up on these clues? Ask them directly about their preferences. The goal is to have communication that leads to answers, solutions, and productive outcomes. And this means adapting to what works best in each scenario, and each relationship.

CHAPTER 9

Mixing Up Meetings and the Power of New Spaces

THE WAY WE WORK is constantly evolving, and a one-size-fits-all physical space doesn't provide us with what we need for the different elements of our roles. Think of a "typical" office with four walls, a stationary desk, a few drawers, two chairs, a computer, some office supplies, and a shared printer that only seems to work from 1:30 p.m. until 1:37 p.m. How can this space inspire creativity while allowing you to have one-on-one conversations, conduct larger meetings, and visualize the flow of the next big project or idea? It can't! We all need different spaces to get the creativity juices flowing and to interact with our colleagues, supervisors, and outside constituents.

Many companies and organizations are changing their structural design to provide these spaces in which their employees engage in conversations, host and hold meetings more effectively, and enhance collaboration and innovation. These tweaks have helped build relationships and communication and enhance productivity.

All organizations have some form of a hierarchy. But we don't have to make them so visually obvious. There are plenty of opportunities to shake things up and give power to people who sometimes feel like they're at the bottom of the food chain. These changes don't have to be earth shattering. They can be simple, and they can happen without big spending by the company.

For example, plenty of times I have been sitting directly across from my boss in their "power chair," trying to engage, and I just haven't felt like I had the power to do so. And it wasn't because they weren't giving me the floor to ask and answer questions or to provide additional feedback, but because there was this wall (the desk) in front of us. The large executive desk felt like a force field that I couldn't cross over. They could lean back in their comfy leather chair or spin around in circles if they wanted, whereas I was on the other side in a semi-uncomfortable non-moving chair, which made it feel like I was about a mile away. This is a classic workspace problem that doesn't need to be fixed with a full-blown renovation.

Although tearing down walls and making big changes may be in the cards for some organizations, others may not have such deep pockets. So, in this chapter, we're going to review both big and small adjustments we can make to our existing spaces, as well as conversations we can have if we're in the market to shake things up entirely. Even minor adjustments to our working spaces give us all the power to drive changes in communication.

Before taking a deep dive into a major reconstruction project, let's start with the basics. These basic changes can come from any member of your organization and don't require a lot of money (if any). These are adjustments that you can implement immediately, and they will have an instant positive impact on the conversations you have with others in your company.

Stand Up

Sitting through an hour-long meeting can be torturous. Similarly, having to wait days for a weekly meeting when something needs to be addressed immediately can be the worst. One of my supervisors handled both of these problems by instituting 15-minute standing meetings during a busy season. We would all gather in his office at the start of the day and chat quickly about what was on the docket, the issues we were facing, and what support we needed. In these meetings, we were open to helping one another and making fast decisions, and we weren't stuck waiting a week to resolve timely issues. Keep in mind that standing meetings shouldn't be more than 15 minutes (no one wants to stand for much longer), should be informal in nature, and can be daily, weekly, or whatever time period is warranted.

Switch Seats

Who said that a meeting with the boss has to mean meeting in the boss's office? If you're a supervisor, suggest meeting in your employee's office. If you're an employee scheduling a meeting, put the location in your office. There's something about sitting in the figurative driver's seat once in a while that helps break down some barriers. This idea, of course, assumes you have an office with a door and aren't in an open floor plan, where meeting will bother the people around you.

If you're working on spicing up a group meeting, try changing up the location and seats. In one of my previous roles, we had two-hour meetings every week in the same room. Although the chairs were comfy and the white boards were handy, the room felt like it was caving in after a while. Managers don't always have to sit at the head of table. They are not your grandparent, and this is not Thanksgiving. A change of venue distributes the power. In the end, it can cultivate some awesome ideas in a new, freeing space.

Move Your Chair

If your desk is sandwiched between your chair and your visitor's, consider moving your chair to the side of your desk so you're almost sitting next to the person you're having a conversation with. When you're speaking with someone in your office, this simple shift of your chair makes the conversation more intimate and starts to break down that perceived force field that you can feel from having the desk in between you and them.

Take Turns Leading

Although this isn't a structural or physical change, giving someone else the opportunity to lead in a meeting can change the dynamics and enhance feedback and discussion. Are there parts of the agenda another employee could lead? Can teams alternate in leading each week? Give people the chance and show that you trust them to take ownership of discussions. This will give other employees confidence in presenting, while giving managers the ability to gauge an employee's leadership development. If you do try this strategy, make sure not to spring it on them at the last minute. Give them notice so they'll have time to prepare.

Now, let's move on to some areas that I would consider middle ground. We're still not knocking down walls, but we are making changes to the way we work that might take a little more time to get used to.

Reshape Your Tables

When we think about people gathering for a meeting and sitting at one large table, it's pretty typically a rectangle or oblong shape. This boardroom-style table provides a head for someone to lead the meeting from, and it can be the most space efficient. Although this style is useful on some occasions, for the day-to-day functions and more casual team meetings, it perpetuates a hierarchical experience. The head of the table tends to be the person leading while everyone else sits around it.

To even the playing field, it's best to find configurations that don't focus on one or a few people. Shapes that are more conducive to creating spaces for more open communication are

Circular. Round tables work well to create a collaborative work environment for a small group of people. Even if it's just two employees, there's no clear divide or emphasis on one person over the other, and no matter where you sit, you're not choosing sides.

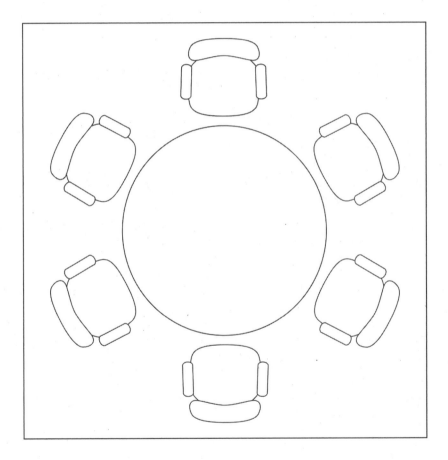

Square. Square tables provide four even sides, and depending on the size, you can fit several in one room. If, at times, you need a more traditional board room for certain events, this style can easily be expanded to a rectangle by adding another table.

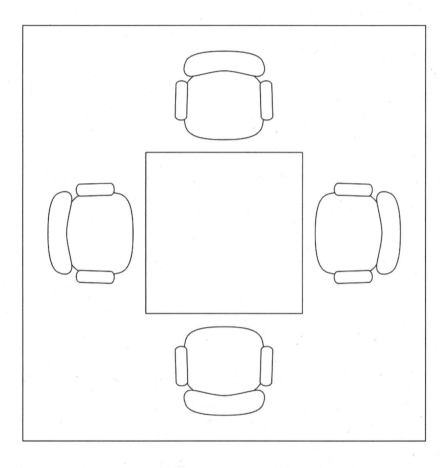

"U" or "C." These configurations work well for presentations, video conferences, small meetings, and workshops. These work best when you're looking to combine presentations and group interactions with discussions so everyone can physically see others in the room.

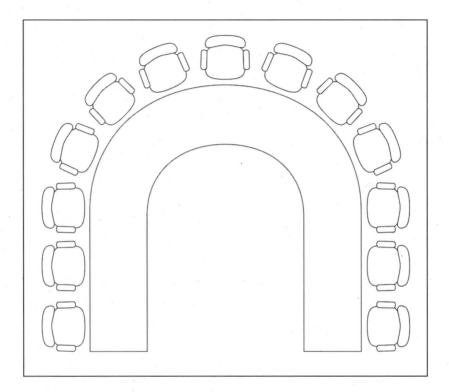

This isn't to say you need to throw all of your rectangular tables to the curb. But if you're looking to update furniture or add some new pieces, the shapes just listed are worth considering instead of always going the regular rectangular route.

Other styles to consider for trainings or company-wide meetings are

School. Smaller rectangle tables with a few seats at each table facing forward. The table allows for participants to take notes, use their devices, and eat while listening to a speaker. This works best for trainings or seminars.

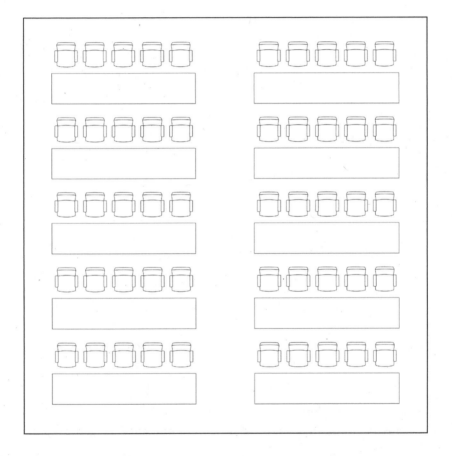

V-shaped. This style is very similar to the school setup, but instead of the tables facing forward, they are angled to the center with an aisle in the middle—making a V shape. This small change in angle allows the person on the farthest end of each row to get a better view of the speaker.

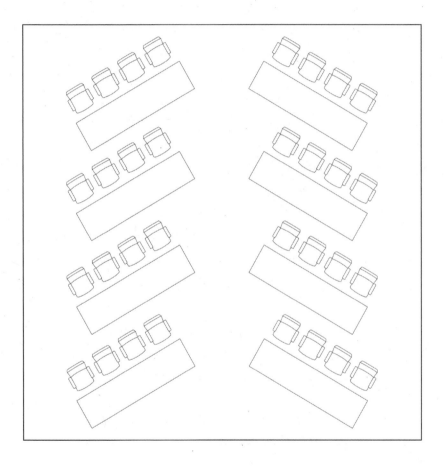

Theatre. This is a row of chairs facing forward with an aisle in the center and space on the sides for people to walk up and down. This setup works for company-wide meetings or larger conferences. But if you're looking for interaction between the attendees or for them to take notes, this isn't the best fit.

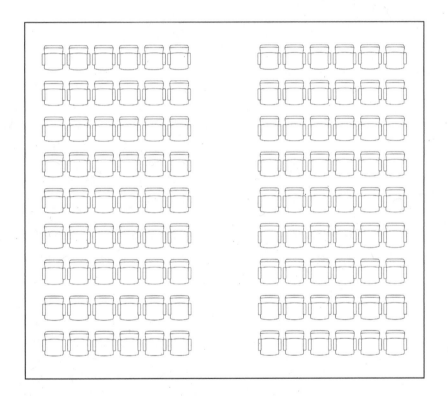

Encourage Shared Spaces

It's so easy for us to stay in one space if we don't have meetings and are buckling down to work through projects. But if everyone has their face down and is on the computer all day every day, we're in trouble. You can make minor changes that provide employees with opportunities to get out of their workspaces and interact with others while still enhancing productivity. These adjustments don't cost a lot and can even wind up saving money.

- Create a centralized location for printing and limit machines in individual spaces.

- Add communal trash and recycling bins to various locations across the office and remove cans from individual spaces so employees need to get up to throw something away.

- Provide coat racks or closets in communal spaces and encourage hanging outerwear in those locations.

- Encourage people to use centralized locations to enjoy their meal by offering tables, chairs, and booths at which people can gather.

- Add inexpensive furniture (like ottomans and high-top tables) in communal spaces and encourage employees to use them for small group conversations.

As with any type of change, it takes time to implement these things into company culture. Throwing a few bean bags in the center of the office won't necessarily bring people to these areas, but if leadership is promoting and using this space more, other employees are likely to follow. Communicate the impending changes by providing the necessary information, and offer a forum in which people can ask questions. This way everyone is well aware of where their trashcans went.

HUMAN CONNECTION

One of the biggest barriers to an open floor model is acoustical interruption. It's important to set precedents and protocols of how you collaborate in a space without interrupting someone else's ability to concentrate. Our company has made an active effort to establish these protocols. If your phone call or conversation is more than two minutes in an open area, we move it to a huddle room, or another enclosed location to be less disruptive. If we're presenting during a conference call or webinar, we use a meeting room. And if we're on a conference call where we won't be talking all that much, we stay in our workplace.

We're also trying to promote the use of our work café by hosting continuing education courses every Tuesday and Thursday in that location. It has sound masking (white noise), a pantry set up with snacks and coffee, catering-sized refrigerators, a mug washer, upholstered steps to sit on, different sizes of tables and lounge seating, and loungers with articulated keyboard trays. We also have click-share to easily share what we're working on with our group. These varied spaces provide options for individuals and large and small teams to collaborate.

AMY GALLAGHER, Senior Interior Designer at Nelson

Add Some Color

The colors of our spaces have an impact on our moods, emotions, productivity, and interactions with others. According to a study from the University of Texas at Austin, employees who work in blue/green, blue, or subtle white spaces experience a higher level of satisfaction in their jobs and have increased performance.[1] Knowing what mood and emotion a color brings is important when you're trying to create an inclusive and productive environment. Below are some other colors to consider when updating spaces:

Red	Soft shades can create a cozy environment.
Orange	Earthy shades can bring feelings of relaxation.
Purple	Muted tones can create an airy atmosphere and richer tones bring thoughts of importance.
White	Tinted and softer shades create a more open and welcoming space.
Yellow	Softer tones can show hospitality and energy.

Knock Down Walls

Knocking down walls, rearranging workspaces, and investing in alternative furniture is no small task or expense. It's not something to be taken lightly and should be carefully considered, researched, and approved. Organizations that value a culture of openness and transparency don't always translate this into their structural spaces. And being able to identify what changes can be made within your organization before making huge adjustments is vital.

Many companies, including Apple and Amazon are spending the time and money to ensure that their spaces encourage conversations and collaboration. But each situation is different, and how you define, and experience, collaboration and innovation will dictate the direction you take. Taking the time to gain a deeper insight into the structural needs of your employees will be well worth the effort.

HUMAN CONNECTION

At my last job, the entire organization moved from an old-school, brick office building into a brand new, modern high-rise. After decades of working in traditional, dry-walled offices, all of the departments were to be moved to an open concept, all-glass environment. It was a big change.

Senior leadership knew there would be resistance and made a lot of effort to ease the transition. They sent out frequent messaging with updates, had open forums for asking questions, and even led hard-hat tours of the new space as it was it being built. They formed different committees open to everyone who wanted to be involved in the process: a community and culture committee for initiatives around creating a positive office culture, an art committee for selecting the art that would be displayed on the walls. And they actively and thoughtfully addressed employees' needs for new tools in order to adjust to the new space—noise canceling headphones for those who needed quiet to concentrate, computer monitor shades for those now in brighter, window-side workspaces.

Of course, there were always going to be employees who were negative—the ones who would complain no matter what. But there was also plenty of positivity and excitement. Yes, most employees were losing their private office spaces and the ability to close a door during a phone call. It was a drastic change in work space. But instead of an outright revolt from the staff, the good attitudes helped drown out the griping ones. Leadership empowered their employees to contribute to their new space, and it really made a difference in the transition.

COLLEEN, Marketing and Communications Professional

Through my conversations with managers and employees, I found a common issue—they lack easy access to spaces for impromptu meetings. Whether they work in a building with private offices, open floor plans, or a combination of both, they do not have many spaces for a few people to gather to have a spur-of-the-moment conversation. Some of the specialty spaces being designed to help organizations with these issues are

Work cafés. These spaces promote social connection in an informal setting. They typically have booths, rectangular tables, and high-top tables where employees can grab lunch and a latte and have a conversation. You can host spontaneous or planned meetings in these more open locations.

Huddle rooms. This is a smaller space for two to five people to gather for a quick, impromptu, and informal conversation. These are not meant for all-day meetings and should have an easy technology hook up with visible instructions for all users popping in and out of the room.

Videoconference space. These larger rooms provide a space for an in-person team to gather and have a virtual conversation with others. A larger screen is placed where everyone in the room can be seen and heard by the virtual participants.

Brainstorm room. Although you can use a huddle room or other location for a quick idea session with a small team, brainstorm rooms can be used for extended periods for larger groups. Participants should be able to write on walls, large note pads, or whiteboards. Additionally, seating should be comfortable, and tech should be available and easy to use.

Work pod/Quiet pod. These individual spaces can be the size of a phone booth. Providing these private options is important when you transition employees to an open office environment. When you ask employees to shift from a private office where they can shut the door to make a call to an open plan; these spaces give them an opportunity to still have some privacy. They provide a private environment in which an employee can take a client or personal call or a visiting remote worker can work for the day. They are not meant as a long-term solution to a private office.

HUMAN CONNECTION

I'm always very leery of **architecture determinism,** the belief that if we change the space, the space will actually change the behavior. It's a yin and yang relationship that requires proactive conversations. What we see over and over again—because people don't have the type of support they need for these physical change conversations—is poor etiquette causing bad behavior. And then those behaviors cause interruptions and distractions and generate noise. The behavior from a cubicle environment is being carried over to open floor models. This change is much more than taking down panels and having people more exposed. It's important to rethink what activities go on and what kind of support those activities require, and then give people more range to roam to different places during the day as opposed to sitting in one place. People are looking for a greater variety of spaces, and that requires a change in the business model to reflect how people think about space and space allocation.

GARY MICIUNAS, Workplace Strategist

Many companies allow employees to reserve some of these spaces in advance, while leaving others open and available for last-minute conversations (like huddle rooms and work/quiet pods). By giving employees a few options, you provide them with opportunities for both scheduled gatherings and impromptu calls or group discussions.

Remember, knocking down walls isn't always the answer, but it can be something to explore as you and your organization think about where communication is now and where you want it to be. You can start off by making small changes to your individual spaces, like coming out from behind that desk! Experiment and see how to change up your interactions, especially if you don't have the power to call for construction. If you're committed, and in a position, to make some larger moves, try bringing in an expert to ensure you're covering your bases. You don't want your employees thinking, "Did they even put any thought into this before making these changes?"

BE HUMAN. ACT HUMAN.

Finding the balance between "we" and "me" is crucial when creating and bringing to life your workspace. Although it's important to have the space to think and work independently, we need to make an active effort to include people and not draw more attention to the hierarchy that exists. Simply moving your chair, changing up the location of your next meeting, or going all out and creating an entirely new space can be effective. But, one thing's for sure . . . if we don't do anything, nothing will change. If you really want to get the conversation going, get rid of the chair, get rid of the table, and get outside of your roles.

PART IV

Be Comfortable with the Uncomfortable

CHAPTER 10

Working with Toxic People

EVERY WORK ENVIRONMENT is not a perfect match of personalities. We've all had that difficult coworker or boss (or potentially have acted like one), and they can make our lives miserable! These are the people who seem to go out of their way to disagree with our opinions and always stir up drama. Although I would love to spend pages ranting about this population, I think it's more important to know who they are and what we can do to make our interactions more productive.

When starting one of my previous positions, I was eager to learn the ropes, navigate the material, and be of help to anyone who asked. But most of the content we needed to know to perform our jobs was not online, in a manual, or documented in any sort of way. The unwritten department policy was that if you wanted to learn, you needed to observe and ask questions of people with institutional knowledge, and then it was sink or swim.

Being the eager person that I am, I asked a coworker a client's question I was struggling to answer on my own. They seemed happy to help and walked me through the response, for which I thanked them, and then I took the information back to my client. Well, it turns out that the information they gave me was *completely wrong*. The client reached out a few days later, confused by my answer, and after additional research and a conversation with my supervisor, we were able to resolve the issue. Although my client was understanding, this incident put not only my reputation on the line, but also my client's trust in our organization. They could have easily walked away and chosen to work with someone else.

Later, I overheard that same coworker talking with someone else about how they gave me the wrong information on purpose to see what I would do. Ever the optimist, I gave them the benefit of the doubt and asked another question later that week, only to find out that they had again given me incorrect information (this time I did additional research before I talked to the client). Sucky, right? It felt horrible to know that someone was outright sabotaging me from the get-go, but I wasn't going to let that get in my way of trying to build a working relationship with them. After this second time, I invited them to lunch to give us an opportunity to start to clear the air. Although they never admitted to giving me the wrong information, we were able to have a civil discussion about the incident. We never became friends or lunch buddies, but we remained professional and generally stayed out of each other's way.

I knew that because my coworker had been there for a long time, they would not be let go, or even disciplined. So, I needed to find a way to work around the situation. And I certainly wasn't going to let it get in the way of my success within the organization. I turned to others as resources and created a manual for new employees to be able to reference. I didn't want anyone to feel stuck, without someone or something to turn to if they had questions.

Unfortunately, my story is not unique. Many people have faced situations in which their coworkers put them down or set them up for failure for their own personal gain. It's hard to get past conversations and situations that make you feel undermined or to shake off someone who seems to always argue just for the sake of arguing. But ultimately, it's important to build a working relationship with these people, if for no other reason than to get your job done without pulling your hair out.

Maybe It's Me?

Before we dive into the types of toxic colleagues and how to engage with them, I'm going to call out the elephant in the room. We've all probably demonstrated a few of these behaviors at some point in time but don't always fess up to it. It's a lot easier to blame other people or assume they're being unreasonable than it is to reflect on our own behaviors. Take some time to do some self-reflection before jumping into conversations with others. You may want to consider:

Conducting a 360 review. These reviews give others the opportunity to anonymously provide insights on your interpersonal skills. They usually include feedback from your manager and peers in a structured online format, giving you a better idea of how others view you professionally.

Asking for feedback. Open yourself up for feedback during one-on-one meetings, formal reviews, or with friends, family, and mentors. Ask what you can do differently to enhance your communication skills and what they've noticed about your communication style. Be open to hearing some things you might not want to hear! And don't get annoyed at someone for sharing their honest opinion. Whether it's going in your ears or not, it's a perception that exists, so try to process what it means and how you might address it.

Self-discovery. Have you found yourself playing the blame game a lot? On more than a few people, and perhaps around the same topic or concern? Have you ever thought that people were just out to get you? For example, do you think that no one can do their job as well as you do yours, regardless of what department they're in? Although such thoughts might not be clear indicators that you're demonstrating toxic behavior, it's something to note if it becomes a pattern.

If you realize you're showing some toxic tendencies, make an active effort to do something about it. As a manager, have one-on-one conversations with your team on how you can best support them individually.

Seek out leadership and communication training both inside and outside your organization, and apologize to those who have been affected by your behavior (refer to chapter 15 for some effective tools). Seek out support from a coach or mentor to help you work through personalized strategies to move past this behavior.

WAYS TO IDENTIFY IF YOU'RE THE TOXIC COLLEAGUE

✔ Conduct a 360 review.

✔ Ask others for feedback.

✔ Spend some time in reflection and self-discovery.

HUMAN CONNECTION

If you find that people always agree with you in meetings, they may be afraid to challenge your position. If your coworkers stop talking when you come near them, they may be uncomfortable around you and may not consider you a part of their inner circle. If you sense any of these warning signs, strive to listen more. Take note of your body language, especially when someone else has something to share with the group. If a coworker approaches you about being difficult, think before you speak. Pause and thank the coworker for sharing her concern. Then, talk about what steps you might take to make things more comfortable. When we take ownership for our role in a relationship, we help open the lines of communication. Try something like: "Thanks for sharing this with me, Suzy. I'm so sorry that you feel that way, as that is not my intent. What could I do differently to make our work relationship smoother?" Then, follow up in a week or so to see if your coworker is feeling more comfortable.

AMY COOPER HAKIM, PhD, Author of Working with Difficult People *and Founder of The Cooper Strategic Group*

The Types of Toxic

Although it can be easy to identify obvious toxic behaviors, like screaming, slamming doors, or even purposely giving out the wrong information—you might be faced with some more subtle ones:

Labelling or generalizing employees. "Of course, the Millennials want a new coffee maker. What unnecessary thing are they going to ask for next?"

Ignoring your ideas. "So anyway, we're going to move forward with my plan since everyone seems to be on board."

Interrupting and never giving others the chance to speak: "Let me jump in, I've had the same experience and think we need to make some changes." Or not giving the heads-up that they have something to say and either talking right over people or talking nonstop.

Patronizing those they feel are less experienced. "For the last 20 years we've been doing it that way, and it's worked fine. Take it from someone with experience, there's no reason to change our protocols."

These behaviors not only destroy relationships, but also make it difficult—if not impossible—to get your work done. Let's look at some types of toxic coworkers and how they may demonstrate these behaviors:

TYPES OF TOXIC EMPLOYEES	DESCRIPTION
The Self-Absorbed	These are the people who always seem to shift the conversations to be about them and can't be bothered with what you have to say. You could be pouring your heart out while they inevitably shift the spotlight back on themselves, making a story or situation about them. They never seem to be attentive to your needs. "It sounds like you're having a rough day, but mine has been crazy too! I just got slammed with two new projects and have no idea how I am going to do everything."

TYPES OF TOXIC EMPLOYEES	DESCRIPTION
The Blamer	They don't take responsibility for their actions and tend to blame others for things not going as planned. Whether it is missing project deadlines or not meeting their goals, it's always someone else's fault they didn't meet expectations. They don't have any plans to change their ways, because it's not their fault. "I haven't had the chance to call the client back because I was pulled into four meetings today and my phone has been ringing off the hook. If I had extra hands around here, this wouldn't be an issue."
The Controller	These are the people that want to control any and all decisions. They will stop at nothing to make sure you agree with their point of view or complete the project in the way they think is best. Your opinion doesn't matter, and it always goes in one ear and out the other. They want to make sure they get the credit for the success. "That's great that you feel that way, but we're going with my plan."
The Dramatizer	Everything is a crisis, and they can't seem to get over the little things. They tend to rant on about something that bothers them and try to bring people into their drama by suggesting they should feel the same way. They can also be the office gossip who walks around recruiting people to be on their side about an issue. "Can you believe that Alexis is making Joe answer the phones during lunch today? That's so ridiculous, doesn't she know how busy he is right now?"
The Complainer	Every job has someone who does nothing but complain! They're exhausting to be around and have no interest in making things better or enacting changes. They just seem to take joy in the griping! They are not out to just get you, they seem to make it a point to criticize everyone's opinions and suggestions and rarely have anything productive to say. This can be through one-on-one conversations or complaint sessions. Or they can be someone who tends to yell publicly in the office. "We've tried that before and it's not going to work."

TYPES OF TOXIC EMPLOYEES	DESCRIPTION
The Saboteur	A person who sabotages coworkers or takes all the credit for their own professional benefit, not working for the benefit of others, but to improve their standing in the eyes of supervisors. They want all eyes on them and will make an active effort to make that happen. My story at the beginning of this chapter gives an example of providing the wrong information for personal gain.
The Critic	Someone who is always critiquing you. Whether it is how you work or who you have lunch with, they always seem to have a suggestion on what you should be doing, and it most likely doesn't affect them in any way. They just want you to know they have a better opinion or way of doing something. "Grant, you know if you just worked with Paul like I suggested, you would have finished this project an hour ago."

Communicating with Toxic Coworkers

Even though each of these categories of toxic colleagues are a little different, you can implement a few strategies in your daily communication to make your interactions more bearable. As much as I would love to wave a magic wand to rid the world of this type of behavior, the only behavior we can control and adjust is our own. Remember, these are people you have to be around and work with every day. They may be very important to how the company functions, so your own success depends on your ability to work with them.

Bring Up Bad Behavior

For the most part, toxic people are not aware that their actions are, in fact, toxic. Their personalities may be based in how they have professionally succeeded to this point in their career. They continue their ways and sometimes wonder why things don't work out, while being completely oblivious to the rolling eyes around the room.

If this behavior impacts your ability to complete your work, and you are looking to change the behavior as opposed to work around it, you can make the other person aware of their behavior. We're not talking about a verbal or physical confrontation—you'll need to find another way to address these coworkers that stifle creativity, don't listen, or aren't open to your ideas and suggestions.

Looking to change someone's behavior is not easy, or sometimes, even possible. But if you want to bring up this behavior with a colleague, try all of the following steps:

Use facts and be specific. Verbatim or as close to word for word as possible, recite what the other person said. Avoid accusatory language that points the finger. Terms like *always* and *never* can make a person feel attacked. Instead, be specific about the time of the incident that you're addressing like "this morning" or "during the meeting." "During our morning meeting when I was providing a suggestion for our new app, you mentioned that we've tried that before, and it didn't work."

Expressing your feelings. Share how this person's behavior made you feel. "I didn't feel that I was given the chance to share my idea fully with the team before you made your comment that ended the conversation."

Providing alternatives. Let them know how you would prefer to work together and ask for their support or alternative suggestions. Try having these conversations in a comfortable, nonstressful environment. Maybe take it outside of the everyday workplace so that you can both focus on the conversation (and not on the tension left in the meeting room). "In the future, I would greatly appreciate you giving me the chance to fully share my ideas to our group before saying whether or not you believe it is a good idea. Is this something you would be able to do?"

HUMAN CONNECTION

Whether we admit it or not, most adults ascribe to a "What's in it for me?" philosophy. So, a difficult coworker is more likely to listen to your ideas if they understand how it will benefit them to do so. Try saying this before offering a suggestion: "I have an idea that I know the boss will really like." Or, "This worked for me when I was at my previous company, so it is definitely worth considering."

If your coworker refuses to let you speak without constant interruption, consider writing down ideas before your meeting, and encourage them to do the same. Then, take turns sharing your ideas as you discuss each one. Don't forget to speak up when there is a break in dialogue. "Good idea, Jim. Here's another angle that I thought of . . . ."

Sometimes, a supervisor might appear to know all of the answers. Even if they think that they are always right, however, they will still want to hear something that will make them look good to *their* supervisor. Try saying this before offering a suggestion: "I know that this works well for our competition, so I think we should see if it could work for us, too." Or, "Mary found great success using this approach."

AMY COOPER HAKIM, PhD, Author of Working with Difficult People *and Founder of The Cooper Strategic Group*

Although it would be nice to be able to have this conversation once and have everything be resolved, it most likely won't be the only time. If you're committed to adjusting this person's behavior to work together better, expect to have a conversation after each instance of this behavior. For example, if at the next meeting you try to bring up another idea and they cut you off, have a similar conversation with this person afterward. It takes conscious effort, time, and persistence to move the needle forward on someone's behavior that they've likely spent years exhibiting. Remember that these behaviors and personalities may be engrained in a coworker's work personality, so they are not going to magically change.

And if you're not their supervisor, they may be resistant to change for someone they don't report to—making it even more difficult for it to stick. But without putting in this effort, you'll feel even more stuck in the mud and powerless. Do your part in trying to make things better.

HUMAN CONNECTION

I ran into a situation in which I was working with an abrasive colleague. Our natural inclination is to avoid these individuals, but I realized that they had the potential to add a lot of value and took a proactive approach to building the relationship.

Our company's culture and core values center around valuing others. So, I forced myself to dig deeper and "peel the onion" as my high school theatre teacher used to say. What were my perceptions of my colleague and what might be driving those perceptions? Was it cultural bias? Differences in communication styles? It is difficult to address interpersonal issues in a meaningful way if we're not willing to do any introspection on our own. Let's face it, sometimes we are the problem, not them. Anyway, after I did this, I realized that I did not know this person well enough to make any kind of determination about them and the way forward.

I scheduled a check-in to get to know them. Rather than delving into any issues immediately, which might have put them on the defense, we chatted about their professional background, their work, what they like about it, and what challenges/pain points they have. I then pushed a little further into the intersection of how my work and my team's work had an impact on theirs to get a sense of what was going well and to find opportunities for improvement.

I learned a lot in that hour-long conversation. We had two very different styles of communication. I'm a bit more diplomatic and they were very direct, which came from a strict upbringing. I also learned more about their personal core values, and at the heart of them are accountability and doing the work correctly, which strongly drives the way they work with others. This really informed the way I now work with them because I realized that there are certain nonnegotiables if we are going to effectively work together.

CHRISTINA MERRIWEATHER, Enrollment Manager

TIPS FOR DISCUSSING TOXIC BEHAVIOR

✔ Share the facts and be specific.

✔ Express your feelings.

✔ Provide alternatives.

So, you've put in the effort and it's not going anywhere. . . . If you're not making progress with your conversations or are looking to move past or around this behavior, it's time to take a different approach. These following suggestions will give you a tool kit for lessening the blow of a toxic coworker.

Don't Take the Bait

I get it, it's hard to give respect when you feel like you're not getting it. But being rude back isn't going to get you heading anywhere in a positive direction. When you take the bait, you're giving them exactly what they're looking for (especially with a toxic person!).

One of the most interesting stories I've heard from an HR manager is their experience working with two employees who got into a physical confrontation (after many previous arguments). One employee had just had enough from his controlling peer who would not listen or take his ideas seriously. He was tired of being pushed around and proceeded to grab his coworker's privates to "show him who was boss" in the middle of the factory assembly floor. Needless to say, he did not handle this situation properly, and as a result, no longer works for the company.

Whether what he was arguing for was right or wrong certainly doesn't matter anymore. You don't have to agree with people, but you should always be respectful. If you have a tendency to flare up and say, or do, things you regret, keep a strategy at the ready:

Take a breath (maybe several). Don't jump right in. Take a moment to collect your thoughts. If you need to, excuse yourself to get some water or use the restroom before moving forward with the conversation.

Create boilerplate responses. These phrases might sound forced, but that's OK! It's way better than stooping to their level. Be aware of your tone and don't be condescending, demeaning, or sarcastic when responding. Try these phrases on for size, "I'll look into that." "Thank you for your feedback." "I appreciate your feedback."

Shift the dialogue. Make an effort to change the direction of the conversation. If someone stole your idea and is trying to play it off as their own, try restating your idea and adding "Here's what I'm thinking . . . ." Then add your strategy and tactics so everyone knows that you have spent time thinking about this. If someone has cut you off, say "Let me finish my point" or "I would like to say something." To shift the dialogue, it's important to be mindful of your tone and share your knowledge without putting the other person down.

Find a Mediator

Sometimes relationships are so damaged that they're seriously getting in the way of work. In this case, reach out to your supervisor and/or human resources to schedule a meeting with a non-biased third-party present to help you clear the air. This helps get both of your voices heard so you can start to get on the same page. This route may also be appropriate if you are not getting a response, or if the same thing keeps happening when you're trying to handle it by yourself.

Ignore Them

This can be tricky if you need to consistently work with this person. If your daily tasks and projects don't typically align with this person's work, try to ignore them. Don't step in the line of fire if you don't have to. When something comes up and you need to work with them, ask for support from your supervisor, who should already be aware of the situation. If they aren't, now is the time to fill them in.

Detach Yourself

All strategies aside, some people just *suck!* I've heard countless stories about employees and bosses who scream when they want something done, don't get their way, or just feel like people aren't listening to what they're saying—like a small child having a temper tantrum. These people can be notoriously hard to work with, and honestly, they will most likely never change this deep-rooted behavior. The best thing to do in these situations is not engage, stay calm, and not try to be the hero (Hint: They're not even listening). The process of engaging is apt to just bring you down and make you feel defeated.

Make a commitment to detach yourself from the behavior and consciously decide that it's their problem, not yours. If it gets over the top or you feel threatened, contact the appropriate person—your supervisor or someone in human resources. This is going to take some serious self-talk to fully commit to, but it is worth the effort. It's hard to remove your feelings from someone else's behavior, but if you know that you deserve better, it becomes a little easier. Practice saying to yourself, "I will no longer be made to feel devalued and unappreciated. I am worthy of respect and appreciation."

Don't Become the Toxic Employee

Don't drag someone else into the mess who shouldn't be involved. Just because you have an issue with a coworker, doesn't mean you should create a coup against them. Bringing other peers into it will not help you in the long run. It can lead to more stress for the people you bring in, make them feel like they need to take sides, or even add more work to their plates in their efforts to help you avoid your peer.

HUMAN CONNECTION

Human Resources wants to know about actions that can impact the company. Many organizations have policies that require employees to immediately report any harassment, bullying, or discrimination. These types of circumstances should not be handled on your own.

For other issues, you want to identify the severity of the situation. If your coworker is providing persistent and unreasonable criticism, insulting or treating you with disrespect, spreading rumors, not following through on tasks, or not listening to your ideas, you can start to address these issues on your own. The first step is to have a conversation with the other person to give them a chance to discontinue this type of behavior. If it continues and your communication methods are not working, bring it up to HR. Although you don't want to be viewed as a tattletale or complainer, when a situation is serious and you are not making progress speaking to the offender, HR can be a valuable resource.

ANONYMOUS, *Human Resource Professional*

BE HUMAN. ACT HUMAN.

Try to give people the benefit of the doubt, even when it's tough. It's important to create the space and opportunities for open conversations, especially with people we don't really want to talk to. We all have a story to tell, experiences that shape us, and personalities that help us stand out. Remember to be kind and assume the best intentions. Spend your energy on empathy and understanding—not anger. Make an effort to address behaviors that are affecting your day to day, but know when there are some things you just can't change. Decide for yourself if you need to escalate an issue, detach from it, or perhaps remove yourself completely from an environment or a person.

CHAPTER 11

Turning Down Ideas, Not People

NOT EVERYTHING WE SAY or do is going to be amazing. And although my grandfather used to love to say, "I'm not always right, but I'm never wrong," well, he was—umm—wrong. You are going to be wrong at some point, and probably more than just once.

However, despite occasionally missing the mark with a game-changing idea, few things are more distressing than someone putting the kibosh on that idea preemptively—before we fully express it, shooting it down without a real explanation. And communicating that an idea or plan is not going to work can be delicate. I get it: we don't want to waste our time tip-toeing around criticism for fear of hurting someone's feelings, but we also want people to know that we heard their idea, listened, and then made a thoughtful decision. It all comes down to how we deliver that message.

I will never forget how rude I was to one of my coworkers during a particular situation at a previous job. Our department had been broken up into smaller groups to complete parts of a larger project. During one follow-up meeting, we came together and shared what we worked on, seeking feedback and buy-in from the larger group. One of my coworkers wanted to do a roleplay for an upcoming training and had spent hours scripting exactly what each of the volunteers would say. I sat there, listened to his suggestion, and said, "I don't like that, I'm not going to do it." Yep, I didn't think his idea would resonate with the clients, made a quick judgment, and shut him down in the middle of the meeting. I outright rejected his idea, which in the end, was the right call, but the way I went about it could have fractured both our relationship and my coworker's confidence.

We left the meeting and I could tell that he was upset. Not only because I was being ridiculously rude, but also because he had spent so much time preparing and was invested in his work. I collected my thoughts and quickly realized that the way I spoke was not only insulting, but that I had done it in front of our whole team. I hadn't let him share why he thought a roleplay made sense in this scenario, nor did I offer alternative suggestions or an explanation of my reasoning for disagreeing.

I waited until the next morning to give him some space and to allow myself to collect my thoughts before I approached the issue. As soon as I stepped into the building the next day, I went to his office and asked if he had a few moments to discuss yesterday's meeting. He kindly agreed, and we went on a short walk together to talk it over. Leaving the office was important; we were equal players in the conversation and finding a neutral location made us both more comfortable. Leaving the scene of the crime, so to speak, took some of the tension out of the air.

I apologized for my negative attitude and for saying no to his idea before he had a chance to explain. I then gave my coworker the floor to talk about his concerns and how my words made him feel. I went on to make a personal promise that I wouldn't insult his or anyone else's ideas in a public forum. And although I would still say no to ideas in a meeting if I thought they might not work, I would do so in manner that did not put the person down—in other words, I would turn down the idea, not the person. I would find a way to voice my dissent in a more diplomatic way and then have a conversation with the person presenting the idea one on one. This dialogue became a game changer in our working relationship.

But not being rude is just the start to diplomatically disagreeing with an idea. Navigating this space and arming yourself with strategies can help you not only avoid burning bridges, but also enhance relationships by sharing your thoughts in a tactful way.

HUMAN CONNECTION

Judgments and harsh criticisms stifle the creative process. It's important to find the positive elements in the original idea while providing gentle constructive criticism and next steps. I've learned that providing specific things to think about and areas to develop can improve the creative process if communicated caringly. I also have asked for permission to provide these suggestions, "Do you mind if I tell you what is good about your idea and what can be improved upon?" "Do you want me to tell you why this might work and why it might not work?"

It's necessary to be trustworthy and respectful in this process as these ideas are often someone's dream. "I like what you've started here, and have you considered this . . . ?" "I apologize in advance if my feedback seems harsh or overly pointed . . . ." This tactful language shows that you are interested in helping them finding alternatives to work through their concepts.

JOHN MCADAM, Business Advisor and Author of The One Hour Business Plan

All Complaints, No Solutions

When we say no or complain about something not being effective, we better be prepared to come up with an alternative solution. In my earlier example, when I told my coworker that I wasn't going to participate in his idea, I didn't offer any viable alternative. I complained because I didn't think it would be an effective way to showcase our point, and I didn't speak in a way that invited others to provide other options. Instead, I could have provided a constructive challenge in which I built on what my coworker said and provided an enhancement to their plan, instead of changing the plan completely. "I think I see where you're going with the roleplays and that you're looking for the participants to act out a scenario to see how the audience would react. Would you consider formulating a roleplay that isn't scripted? Perhaps we could provide them with a prompt or let them choose a scenario that they're currently facing? This could help them take it one step further."

The tweaking of my phrasing would have allowed for a conversation about why they chose to script the roleplays and potentially move the needle toward doing something different. A flat out, "No! I'm not going to do that," or "That's not going to work," will not create a constructive conversation. If something isn't going to work out, or if you don't agree with a proposed idea, provide an alternative to the suggestion. Just saying you don't like something, or that you don't want to do it, isn't an answer, and ultimately, if you handle things this way, you end up portraying yourself as someone who isn't open to new ideas and different perspectives.

HUMAN CONNECTION

When our office was bought by a younger doctor, we went through a lot of changes. One of them was upgrading the technology so patients could schedule their own appointments online and shifting from paper to electronic records. In an industry where a lot of offices still use paper records and are only being reluctantly dragged kicking and screaming into a digital world, this move was unusual. The doctor, my new boss, also falsely assumed that because he was comfortable and proficient with technology, our staff would be also.

The technology platform was new to all of the front desk staff, including myself, and we were just provided with the training material with no formal review of how to use it. From the start, I knew this was going to be difficult as the system was unforgiving of simple errors and very time consuming to use, even for a simple task. It also did not meet our needs and the doctor's expectations were unrealistic. Unfortunately, he chose the platform without asking the staff for input and assessed it based on tasks he had never performed.

After using it for a few months, he realized that the platform he chose was not meeting expectations. Instead of looking into alternative options on his own, he is now involving our staff in the process so he can understand how we use it and ensure that it can meet his expectations for transferring data.

ANONYMOUS

Stop Using Terrible Phrases

Be honest: Have you ever been the one to shoot an idea down in front of others? The one who made someone feel uncomfortable about something they worked on? You're not alone! But, here's the deal: there are ways to say you don't like something without immediately pushing people away and stifling their creativity. Take it from me and learn from my mistakes. And remove these phrases from your vocabulary:

- "That's the way it's always been done."
- "That's just the way we do things."
- "That's the way it is."
- "Don't fix something that isn't broken."
- "Figure it out."
- "No." (When said before really hearing someone out.)

You may have seen these in an email before, or maybe you've even had the pleasure of being shot down in person—and better yet, in a room full of your colleagues. (Fun, right?) But at the end of the day, these are just rude phrases for telling someone no. So, let's break them down a little bit to give you a better idea of why they suck, and then we'll talk through alternatives.

"That's the way it's always been done." "We've always done it this way." "That's the way it is." "That's just the way we do things." These similar phrases tell the person that you're not open to new ideas. It's a cop-out answer with no explanation. And who is this "we" that we're talking about? Is it you? The organization? Everyone? This does not explain why their idea isn't going to work and why you're not going with it. Instead, try providing the following information:

What we do	Explain the process, the role, or the scenario in detail.
How we do it	Review how this actually gets done.
Why we do it	Explain why you do it this specific way.
Address why you can't try this new way.	Explain what might be difficult with the newly proposed way, and what issues you see causing roadblocks.

"I appreciate your suggestion, Todd. We have a tight deadline with this project and several departments are involved. We've communicated our current plan to all parties, and it assures that we will be on schedule and within budget. Although we can't make a change in plans for this project, let's discuss your idea in full detail later, as we have several similar initiatives coming up. What does your schedule look like next Friday at 1:00 p.m.?"

Make it clear that you appreciate creative thinking for new solutions, explain why their idea won't work in this instance, and offer a specific time to talk about how it could be developed elsewhere.

"Don't fix something that isn't broken." This phrase suggests that everything is fine with a process and there is no need to ever evaluate or create something more efficient or effective. It also shows we might be too lazy to change things up and try something new. An employee isn't coming to you because the current way of doing things is not working but because they think it can be enhanced to better meet or exceed the needs of others. Using a phrase like this is a turn-off, especially for Millennial and Gen Z employees who grew up learning through technology. We can always do something to enhance a process; this just might not be the right time and place to make that change. "Blair, thank you for your suggestion for improving the response rates for our client surveys. Although I agree that your method is something to explore, it's not something we have the resources to dedicate to at the moment. Let's get together offline after the meeting to talk through alternative budget options, timelines, and resource allocation."

"Figure it out." This reply often comes after someone asks for help. Although I am sometimes a fan of a sink-or-swim approach, having people do certain things on their own without any guidance or resources is usually not the best option.

■ Provide resources (online manual, video tutorials, links).

- If you're unsure of the answer, suggest an alternative person to whom they should direct the question.

- Be supportive.

"Darla, I understand that you need help learning how to use our phone system and with forwarding calls. I would suggest reaching out to Brandon because he is a wiz with our phone system. We also have a video library that will show you step by step how to use it; I will forward you the link."

"No" (When said before really hearing someone out). I am a believer that "No." is a complete sentence and an appropriate response for certain situations (like if your kid asks you if they can go to the 84th kids' birthday party of the summer—just say no and move on). But in the workplace, it's different. We need to take a few minutes and address the "why" *after* that person has spoken. Don't be one of those people who already has an answer in their head before someone has given their thoughts—not even listening to what they have to say. Those in-one-ear-and-out-the-other people aren't building relationships. They're just frustrating others around them. "Eric, I understand what you're saying, but that expense is not something that we can commit to. We have two large events this quarter and the soft serve ice cream machine doesn't fit into our budget."

HUMAN CONNECTION

In my first company, I had a lot of autonomy. As long as my sales numbers were high, I didn't have to get ideas approved first. Then when I switched companies, my new boss wanted to go in one direction, and I wanted to go in another. I chose my direction and thought that if I was successful, I could change his mind. Although it was the right direction, it was the wrong approach. I didn't do what he wanted at all and assumed that the higher sales numbers would be enough. He didn't change his mind, and he almost fired me.

I learned that if I disagree with my boss, I can't just do what I want to do and ignore him. If you disagree with your boss, you should make an argument for another approach. If they say no, you can discuss it one more time, but then after that, you have to drop it and try it their way first. Try your best to make their idea work, or they will blame the failure on your poor execution. Your boss needs to see their vision happen. If this way doesn't work, it's important not to say, "I told you so" or take the blame for their vision not working out. You can now restate your case for a new approach moving forward.

JAMIE LIBROT, Director of Talent Management and Global Strengths Leader

The "Just Because" Mindset

Although your opposition to someone's idea may have made sense at that time and place, it's OK to change your mind later. Listen openly to new data and information presented, and make a logical and factual opinion as things change. It's not about losing or giving in, it's about taking your ego out of it and making the best decisions for your organization and team.

BE HUMAN. ACT HUMAN.

It's OK to say no. What's not OK is being rude, snarky, or inconsiderate of others and what they're bringing to the table. Ultimately, it all comes down to how you approach the situation. If someone is sharing a new way that you don't agree with, hear them out anyway. Listen to what they have to say and then talk through it. Everyone deserves the opportunity to share their ideas and not be blown off. In the long run, this adds to a culture of free and open idea sharing—because we really don't want people to be afraid to speak up.

CHAPTER 12

Saying No and Setting Boundaries

INEVITABLY, YOU WILL have moments when saying no to a coworker's idea is the only real option for next steps. Maybe it's just not a plausible concept or plan, or maybe you just don't have the capacity in your workload to help see it to fruition.

For these reasons and more, you may find yourself in a potentially awkward situation. But earning a reputation for being a naysayer or an "I just don't have time for this" colleague (hair toss and sigh optional) is not a reputation you should desire. On the flip side, trying to be a hero and taking on more work than you can handle isn't a good idea either—for you or your company.

Early on in your career, it's important to establish yourself as someone who completes work and is a go-getter. This is also the case when you're new to a company or team and want to prove your worth. But there are going to be times when you cannot say yes—times when you logistically cannot take on more work, and if you did, the quality of the other work (and your personal life) would be diminished. So, how do you say no without coming across as a bad team player, disgruntled, or like someone who's just looking to get out of work?

HUMAN CONNECTION

I had been working in the International Programs office of a small college for several years. When the Dean of Students (DOS) announced his departure, the assistant dean (ADOS) took on his role on an interim basis. The ADOS, whom I did not report to, had been handling international student visas, and she did not have the capacity to continue once she took on the interim duties. I volunteered to help, and for two years, I managed my previous workload in addition to this large responsibility and other ad-hoc assignments without any raise, added budget, or additional support.

When we hired a new DOS, the interim person went back to being ADOS, while I maintained the responsibility of international student visas. She wanted me to keep it so that she could focus on other areas.

At the same time, the Associate Dean of Faculty (ADOF) was promoted to Dean of Faculty (DOF) and became my new boss. The newly appointed DOF had me take on parts of his old role, which were beyond the scope of my normal duties and had a learning curve. At this time, I now had my original responsibilities, the international student visas, and several new responsibilities from my boss. I asked my boss for additional personnel support so that I could continue to perform this work and the new projects he assigned to me. However, due to the lack of budget, my request was declined.

Although it was hard for me, I knew I had to speak with the ADOS about taking back the responsibility of the student visas. I could not continue to perform the responsibilities assigned to me under my job function, while also focusing on a critical function in the student visa process. I knew if I kept it on my plate, my other work would suffer, and I didn't want to cause potential issues with the student visas. Ultimately, the ADOS took back the responsibility, allowing me to focus on my other tasks. Although I feared the professional impact of telling someone I could not handle the additional workload, I knew the end result would benefit my department and my personal well-being.

ANONYMOUS

Don't Say Yes When You Really Mean No

There have been so many times when my mind is saying no, but my mouth blurts out yes to a colleague. It's just my natural reaction when someone asks me to do something, whether I want to do to it or not. It can happen because I feel bad saying no, or because I don't want to disappoint them. But if you mean no, it's important to not say yes. You don't want to get the reputation for committing to something and not following through. And you don't want to take something on when you know that your mental and physical health will suffer as a result.

If you're not ready to take the full trip into No Town, provide alternative solutions to help your coworker complete their project by suggesting

Qualified individuals who may be able to assist. "I am working on a few time-sensitive assignments right now, but Jen would be a great person to ask as she is working on something very similar."

An alternative timeline where you may be able to get involved (if your schedule clears up). "I'll be conducting two out-of-town trainings over the next three weeks. If this portion of the project can wait until I get back, I can help then." "I need to finish this assignment by 1 p.m. today, but I can circle back to you at 2."

With that said, don't just try to be nice by saying you'll help later if you know that you won't be able to. Things come up, and we can't predict the future, but don't just prolong your no by delaying with empty yeses. In the long run, it's much easier to be honest than to keep putting someone off when your answer was always going to be no. "I will be out of the office conducting trainings over the next three weeks. I know there is a lot at stake with this project and I cannot give it my full commitment, and you deserve nothing less than that. May I suggest reaching out to Tom in accounting, as he has had experience with this before."

Finding Your Go-To Phrases

When your boss comes to you with another project at the eleventh hour and you're already swamped with another deadline, you can't just say, "No, I don't feel like it," or "No! You're driving me nuts. Why do you always wait until the last minute?" Saying no to a supervisor can be difficult because you don't want to come across as someone who isn't hardworking or willing to go the extra mile for your team. You want to be perceived as someone who can be counted on and who is an asset to the company.

But there are going to be times when taking on another project or joining an additional committee is just not feasible given your current workload. Having some phrases in your back pocket will help make this no easier when your boss puts you on the spot.

- "Thank you for thinking of me for this project, but I am currently working on the Griffin assignment that is due to our client by Friday morning at 9 a.m. Is this new project a bigger priority? If so, I can ask Laurie to help me with these two assignments to ensure they get done on time."

- "That sounds like an interesting project, but if I take it on, I will not be able to complete the Watershed assignment by the deadline. Which one is more pressing and needs immediate attention, and which one can hold out for another week?"

- "I know this project is really important and you need extra hands, but I am currently overextended with Project Cornucopia. Is there a specific part that you especially need assistance with? I don't think it would be wise of me to commit to working on the entire project until this other assignment is complete next Friday."

This type of phrasing allows your supervisor to take charge and decide what should be prioritized. In this conversation, they might ask you to stop one assignment to begin another. Before you do that, you want to make sure you're both on the same page.

Supervisor: "Tracy, I need you to shift gears and put a hold on the Star assignment and start working on the Moon project."

You: "I only have one more day worth of work for the Star assignment. Do you still want me to immediately start working on the Moon project?"

Supervisor: "Yes, the Moon project is our top priority and should only take two to three days. After you're finished, please go back to complete the Star assignment."

You: "Thank you for clarifying. I will immediately start on the new project."

· What if the ask is coming from a peer from within or outside of your department? Although they might not be pulling rank for their request, it's still important to show respect. Here are some no phrases to try out for those situations:

- "I appreciate being invited to join your new committee, but I am overextended at the moment."

- "I'm working on a few time-sensitive projects right now, but you may want to reach out to Charles, as he's mentioned wanting to get more experience in this area."

- "Thank you for thinking of me! But I think Cherie would be more suited for this assignment. She has been working on a very similar project with another client and has received positive feedback. I would be happy to connect the two of you and schedule a meeting if that would be helpful."

- "Thank you again for thinking of me; however, this is not an area in which I will be able to assist you as my interests lie in other areas."

- "That sounds like a lot of fun, but I have a prior commitment and will be unable to make it."

- "Thank you for the invitation, but I have a previous family commitment and will not be able to attend."

Being clear, concise, and direct allows you to specifically share what you're working on right now and why you can't take on something new. Remember these components when saying no:

COMPONENTS OF SAYING NO

✔ Show appreciation for being asked.

✔ Provide an explanation of why taking this on would be difficult.

✔ Ask for support in establishing priorities (if appropriate).

✔ Use proactive and direct language.

Although the focus of this chapter is on saying no, I think it's also good to have some go-to phrases and tactics ready for when you're the asker. If you're finding yourself in a position where a coworker or supervisor isn't using the components just discussed, and they leave you wondering why they turned you down, you can take initiative by

Being prepared. If you're asking people to add something to their plate, understand what's already on it. What big projects do they have lined up? When is their busy time? Do they have scheduled time off already on their calendar? Understand your starting point so you know what areas to bring up during your initial or follow-up asks.

Trying again another time. Maybe they were in a bad mood or felt overwhelmed in the moment. Circle back for your ask when their schedule is a bit clearer or they've had their morning caffeine. Just make sure you're not being pushy or seem to be waiting outside their office every time they come back from a meeting. It really might have been a no, regardless of their caffeine intake.

Asking for an explanation. This isn't about accusing or blaming them for not taking on your ask. It's about understanding why and making alternative plans if you get a flat-out no without explanation. "Thank you for getting back to me. I am trying to put together a high-quality team for this difficult project, and your name was on top of my list. Can you elaborate as to why you will not be joining? If it's a matter of timing, I may be able to move some things around, so it better aligns with your other responsibilities." However, be mindful that your line of questioning isn't to make the person feel bad about saying no (or to talk them into saying yes), but to get a better sense of the other factors at play.

Requesting recommendations of people and resources. If they've made it clear that they're either not interested or don't have the capacity—ask for other options. "I appreciate your honesty. Can you recommend someone else for the committee that you believe has the capacity, interest, and knowledge to take this on?"

Not taking it personally. A professional no is not personal. It's about someone's ability to take on something else (based on their workload or otherwise), and not about how much they do or don't like you. "I appreciate your honesty and I hope we have the opportunity to work on a similar project in the future."

STRATEGIES FOR FOLLOWING UP WHEN SOMEONE SAYS NO

✔ Be prepared to explain what you're asking them to do.

✔ Try again another time.

✔ Ask for an explanation.

✔ Request recommendations of people and resources.

✔ Don't take it personally.

BE HUMAN. ACT HUMAN.

If you can't take on another project because you feel like you're going to lose it, respectfully turn it down. Be honest about where you are, what support you need, and be sure to give a respectful response. It can be hard to say no, especially when you want to help your coworkers and impress your boss. But for the sake of your work quality (and your sanity), sometimes you have to make a humble pass.

Part V

The Power of
Relationship Building

CHAPTER 13

Being Present, Being Accessible

ACCESSIBILITY ISN'T JUST being there physically. We have to be mentally and emotionally open—in an authentic way that doesn't immediately set off someone's BS meter. One of the biggest complaints I hear from my corporate clients is that they lack access to leadership. People can easily feel that there is a wall between them and us and become further and further removed from the vision and mission of the organization. When we don't get some type of face time with the people at the top, it's hard to feel connected to what we're working so hard for.

Being present and accessible can be hard. As a manager, it can feel like a burden to get out from behind your screen when meeting requests are never ending and email notifications won't stop dinging. But if we don't make an active effort to acknowledge the people who make up the organization, they will start to look for other jobs with companies where they feel seen and heard.

One of the biggest barriers that perpetuates the feeling of them and us is of our own making. We get so caught up in the day to day that we don't always see the people who keep our company above water. We don't give them the chance to ask questions, be listened to, and feel valued. Being accessible and present, even for 30 minutes a week, is a great place to start. And it is especially powerful for leaders.

Every member of the organization should know who the senior leadership is, a little bit about them, and more than just what their faces look like from the company website. The human connections we make helps shift our mentality from "work is a place I need to be," to "work is a place where I want to be." OK, so work will never be as desirable as an island vacation, but you get the gist. Feeling connected to the those we work with and for makes us feel connected to our work—and that's a positive daily force.

Now, if you're envisioning a montage of kissing babies and giving everyone a handshake or fist bump—that's not what I'm talking about. I'm simply talking about being more present and reachable. Not just to the people who sit in on the board meetings, but to the people who make the daily grind happen.

In one of my previous roles, the senior leader made it a point to go on an annual office tour. Everyone lined up in the hallway as she walked around, she shook everyone's hand, and then we took a group photo. I'll admit, this wasn't the type of interaction I was looking for. It felt like a weird, surface-level interaction that was done just for show. There was no conversation, just a bunch of people in an awkward wedding-style receiving line.

Don't be that kind of leader. Don't let those BS meters flare up when you enter a room. Be both physically and emotionally present for the people who work with and for you. Don't just check off a box. Actually care to engage.

Serve Lunch, Not Speeches

In one of my previous roles, one of our executives made it a point to schedule a luncheon once a month with 25 members of the organization. An email was sent around, and anyone could sign up through an online form. The executive's assistant chose at least one representative per department, and if you weren't chosen that month, you had the opportunity to sign up for the following month. The goal was to have anyone who wanted to meet him to have the opportunity to do so. We're talking entry-level through executive, all levels and all departments.

And this wasn't your typical lunch where you just sat there, ate, and then left. This was a roundtable conversation. The buffet-style catered lunch was set out, we grabbed our food, and then we grabbed a seat at a circular table.

The executive host sat at the table, next to his fellow members of the organization and with a full view of each staff member who was present. He introduced himself in a non-elevator-pitch way and gave us each the opportunity to give an introduction. He talked about what he liked to do for fun, his kids, what drew him to the organization, and what he was excited about in the upcoming month. Then it was an open floor for anyone to ask questions. Topics ranged from improvements needed in the building to his favorite place to grab coffee.

Not only was this an opportunity to get some face time and ask questions that we normally wouldn't get to ask, but we also were able to meet people from all over the organization. This informal setting helped us build more trust with an executive member and air anything we wanted to be heard. No question was turned away, nor did we feel judged (and the free lunch wasn't a bad perk either!).

Livestreaming Leadership

Although it may be feasible for some to block out an hour a month for something like an executive luncheon, it might not be as convenient for others. Likewise, your organization may not have the space for it, or the budget. Another method might be to do a video series with different members of the executive team, the people we tend to see less than anyone else in the organization. I'm not talking about a full feature film here, just a short video (two to ten minutes) that gives people a better understanding of who they are working with and for. This isn't a sales pitch. It's just about communicating a real message in an accessible format.

Prior to filming the video, send an email with a survey giving staff the opportunity to ask questions for a senior leader to answer. Providing staff with a brief bio of the leader beforehand and the responsibilities of that individual will enhance the quality and depth of questions. If you have the technical capabilities, stream the interview live, and then host it on an internal network for all to view later. If you don't, shoot it on a smartphone and distribute however is easiest—no need to get fancy. The key is to actually get to know the people who run the company, not just see their name and headshot.

You can even take this one step further—depending on the information discussed and in what format—and share the Q&A on your company website. This can also help bridge the gap between prospective and current clients, bringing them in on the experiences within the organization. A logo or a slogan doesn't build trust, but a person, an interaction, or an experience will.

HUMAN CONNECTION

In my former company, there was a requirement to have a career development discussion with each of your direct reports along with the performance evaluation process, twice per year. There was an additional option referred to as a skip-level meeting, where you could choose to meet with the direct reports of your direct reports for an individual career development discussion.

My personal practice as a senior executive was to actively schedule skip-level meetings with as many staff on my team as possible. This was an infrequent opportunity for them to get to know a senior leader and realize that everyone at all levels of the organization is just another human being. It was not unusual for me to have over 150 of these one-hour conversations in a given year as I would also schedule them with our global employees when I traveled to their offices. They were an opportunity for each of us (the staff member and I) to learn more about each other, personally and professionally. Although the discussion centered on the staff's education, career experiences, and future aspirations, we also spent time on personal interests.

These conversations helped the senior leadership team develop networking opportunities for staff, and recommend ways they could improve job performance and position themselves for future success. But most importantly, it developed individual connections so we could have a comfortable discussion if we met in the hallway or at lunch. It provided me with information about who might be ready for future projects or challenging assignments. It also helped me develop ongoing relationships so I could continue to mentor individuals as they moved throughout the organization and enhanced their career.

ANONYMOUS, Senior Financial Executive in the Financial Industry

Establish an Accessibility Protocol

In several of my jobs, my bosses were not consistently available. They were either constantly traveling or in and out of meetings. For the most part, this didn't impact the daily function of my job, but it did make it difficult when I had questions or was learning something new. During such times, I quickly became frustrated and felt unsupported. I didn't know when I was going to be able to have my questions addressed and I didn't want to leave my clients hanging with no answers.

Now when I work with clients, I suggest having an initial conversation where both the supervisor and the employee sit down, at least quarterly, to identify what accessibility means to them and how best to communicate with one another. This is where you have a conversation about

The best way to communicate with one another when you have questions. For urgent questions, should we email, text, or call? If a non-emergency question arises, how can we get in touch with one another, and what is the expected response time?

An emergency action plan for issues that need to be addressed immediately. Discuss potential scenarios that may occur (or have occurred)

within your roles and triage how you will get in touch with one another to find a solution. During a time when someone is inaccessible, who will be the alternative point of contact?

Having an initial meeting to discuss this gets everything out in the open about the accessibility of the supervisor and the expectations of the employee so that everyone is on the same page.

Open Office Hours

Days and even weeks can go by in which we don't see the people we work with and for—even if they're in the office next to us. When we keep our heads down looking at our screens and we run around from meeting to meeting, it can be hard to get face-to-face time with our managers or employees. One of my favorite go-tos to help solve this issue is having open office hours.

If you're physically located in an office with your employees, set aside a time period (for example, Mondays from 9 to 10 a.m.) when your door will be open, and anyone can walk in with a question. If you're in a virtual space, take this time to be online on your organization's designated sharing and video-conferencing platform.

Communicate your open office hours to your staff so they know that they have access to you during that time. If you're on vacation or have a meeting outside the office, let your staff know that you have rescheduled your hours to another day, and if need be, to the following week. When you set aside a specific time, it eases concerns when you're not available, because your team knows that at least once a week they can get face time with you to ask a question or review material.

Here's the deal though: it's one thing to say "we have an open-door policy" and another to actually have one. Just because you leave your door open doesn't mean people feel welcome to walk through it. Let's say Suzanne walks up to your office—door wide open—but you remain head down, completely engrossed in your work. When she approaches, you continue to read your email and don't look all of the way up. What do you think Suzanne will do? Well, she has a few options: she can walk in and take a seat, stand in the doorway until you notice her, knock on the door, cough loudly until you hear her, or walk away. If you haven't established a come-in-and-take-a-seat kind of culture, Suzanne is most likely not going to feel comfortable interrupting your mid-email gaze.

In such a situation, a simple hand gesture waving them in or looking up for a second to say, "Come on in and have a seat, I just need to finish this one thing," acknowledges their presence and gives them the heads-up that it might take a minute until they can have our undivided attention. When we have the door open and have a policy for people to come in, but when they take us up on this and then we immediately ignore their presence (or worse: shoo them away), they're most likely not going to come back. And this means we miss a critical opportunity to develop a strong, communicative relationship with our employee.

If you're working through a project that needs your undivided attention, shut the door, put a "do not disturb" notification on your office messaging system, and block off your calendar. You can even reach out to your administrative assistant and give them the heads-up that what you're working on might take an hour and you'll be fully tied up during that time. If you don't have an administrative assistant or haven't talked to your supervisor about whether or not shutting the door is OK, start the conversation. "Mathew, I have a few big projects I'm working on and want to give them my undivided attention for the next few hours. Are you OK with me shutting my door so I can focus?"

Sometimes we forget to shut the door, and that's OK too! Just say to Suzanne, "I want to make sure I can dedicate to our conversation fully, can I circle back to you in 30 minutes?" Then actually go back to Suzanne's office in 30 minutes. If you need to, set a timer or a reminder on your calendar so you don't forget. Don't make a promise of accessibility and not deliver.

Walk the Halls

Get out of your office and walk down the hall and check in with your staff at least once a week. Not in a hovering, micromanaging way, but in a "Hi, I know I have been tied up and wanted to see what I can do to support you," kind of way. If you're not sure how to start the conversation, look for context clues in their workspaces. This could be pictures of their kids, dogs, or a funny sign sitting on their desk. "Henry, your dogs are adorable. How old are they?" "Garrett, that looks like a fun family vacation, where did you go?"

Employees tend to go to their supervisor's office, but it doesn't always happen the other way around. And it should! Show your face around the office and say hello to the people who work with and for you.

Hit the Lunchroom

This goes for anyone in the organization, including leadership. Instead of eating at your desk, sit in the common area with your team and don't talk about work. No one always wants their boss watching over them, but if you're up for having a conversation about the latest TV shows, the new restaurant in town, or a book you loved—most people would be in. Just be yourself and let people get to know you outside of your work persona. They will feel more comfortable when they need to ask questions because they'll see you as more approachable.

Celebrating What Matters

I'm one of those people who's a sucker for birthdays. You know, the one who will decorate your desk, buy you a birthday coffee, and put a card in your mailbox. I get equally invested when someone has earned a promotion, is having a rough day, or when they went out of their way to do something nice for me. Taking the time to acknowledge someone during their special (or even frustrating) event, whether it's big or small, means something. It shows you're paying attention and that you care.

To avoid the "oops, I forgot your birthday" moments, make a note on your calendar and set it as a reoccurring event so you remember. Set a reminder on your calendar for events in the future that an employee mentioned are important to them. If someone mentions their favorite coffee or candy during a random conversation, write it down so you won't forget to add it to their holiday or "just because" gift. You can create a spreadsheet, add it to your meeting notes, or put it in the notes section of your phone. Do whatever helps you remember these little details that mean so much to them.

HUMAN CONNECTION

As a manager and business owner, it's important to be invested in what you do. I still get excited when I secure a client on a TV news show and it fuels me to work harder. I try and use this excitement to influence my employees to also secure press for our PR clients. I want them to actually see why the passion is so important.

Being genuine and having heart goes a long way. Don't just tell your employees you care, actually show them by celebrating with them. Whether it's through a financial incentive, by cheering them on, or by taking them out to celebrate a big win, let them know that you're committed to their success. If your team believes in you and your mission, they will work harder to ensure they make your company a success.

JEN SHERLOCK, President of Jenna Communications

These small acts of kindness make you more accessible, both physically, as you're handing someone something or telling them how awesome they are, and emotionally. You show that you're listening to what matters to them, and that you care about their personal and professional success.

Inaccessible? Over-Communicate It.

Communication can build trust and make employees comfortable. It shows that we're putting ourselves out there and that we're providing information that we believe is valuable to someone else. When we don't communicate, it can leave people around us confused, lost, and feeling underappreciated.

One of the most overlooked pieces of information that we can forget to communicate is when we're taking vacation and sick days. As an employee, you most likely need to request time off from your supervisor, either through an internal system or through a documented conversation. If you're a supervisor and don't report to someone directly, it's still essential to have that exchange. You're not asking or requesting permission, but you're letting your team know that you won't be available for the day, and if anything goes off the rails, who they should contact. Someone from your staff should always be available to reach out to in urgent situations. Without this, people tend to panic.

I will never forget the first time I was sick in one of my roles. I was working at a college at the time, and I got slammed with the flu and could barely make it out of bed, let alone to work. I had never called out before, never asked how to do it or who I should call to do so. Should I call my supervisor? The front desk? My colleagues I had meetings scheduled with? Or someone else? Since I didn't have access to student information on my personal computer, I chose my supervisor and left a voicemail and sent an email. Well, my supervisor was in meetings all morning and didn't have the chance to check her messages until lunch. As a result, my morning student appointments showed up because they hadn't heard otherwise. They were disappointed to find out that I was out for the day and confused as to why no one had let them know. I was frustrated by the way I handled situation. Not only had I not asked about the correct protocol ahead of time, but I didn't confirm that someone else in the office had gotten my message.

So, who should I have called? My answer now: everyone! Learn from my flu-induced blunder, and make sure you discuss the best way to communicate that you will be out sick before you're actually sick. Is it via email, text, or a phone call? With one simple email where you copy all the appropriate parties, you can let everyone know that you will be out sick that day.

If you take it one step further, you can cancel the meetings you had on the calendar, so it automatically sends those individuals an additional notification. Don't leave people hanging and thinking you're accessible when you aren't. Communicate, and then communicate again, that you're out sick and won't be available that day.

In one of my other previous roles, I once walked down the hall to ask my supervisor a question and was told by a neighboring officemate that he wasn't coming in that day. He had said goodbye to her on the way out the day before with a "See you Thursday" . . . on a Monday. My coworker was thrown off and asked for clarification. Our supervisor said that he forgot to add a professional development conference to his schedule and would be out the next few days. Not only was that frustrating because my question had to go unanswered, but we also had a meeting with him on the books for that day. A meeting that was still on the calendar and had not been cancelled.

This lack of accessibility in the immediate moment was frustrating, but the lack of respect he showed by not letting our team know of his absence put a strain on his relationship with us. This situation is not unique; this happens all the time. We get busy and forget what we communicated and what we may have left out.

After the incident, I initiated a conversation with our group on how to communicate our days off. We decided that we would block off our individual calendars, let the front desk know, and tell our team and anyone involved in our projects in advance of planned time off. An out-of-office message would be placed on our voicemail, email, and internal messaging system. It would be 100 percent clear from all angles.

If we were out of the office for work and would be in a different time zone, we shared the time difference between our new location and the central office in our out-of-office correspondence. This made it easier for both internal and external stakeholders to not only reach us, but also to understand why it might take us a little longer to respond.

If you don't have a handy email or voicemail ready, try these:

Out-of-Office Email Templates

Thank you for your email. I am currently traveling to our Brussels office (six hours ahead of EDT). Although I will be answering emails, please note that some of my responses may be delayed due to the time difference.

Thank you for your email. I will be out of the office until (date) and will read and respond upon my return. If this matter needs immediate attention, please reach out to (name) and (email address).

Thank you for your email. I will be out of the office until (date) and will read and respond upon my return. If your matter requires immediate attention, please see your contact point below:

Sales Inquiries: Jane, 555-555-5555, jane@sales.com

Product Orders: Bob, 555-555-5553, bob@sales.com

Out-of-Office Voicemail Template

You have reached (name). I am currently out of the office and will be returning on (date). I will not be checking my voicemail during this time. If you need immediate assistance, please call (name) at (phone number).

As a manager, you also want to notify the person you're leaving in charge during your absence to let them know that they are, in fact, in charge. I've unknowingly been the point person for other managers who were on vacation, and it can be extremely confusing when you're trying to triage incoming calls and emails without the heads-up. Again, when it comes to stuff like this, too much communication is way better than too little. Always make sure everyone is in the know.

Make an Accessibility Plan

With employees working in various time zones with clients from all over the world, it's important to have an accessibility plan in place. If your physical office closes at 5 p.m. but your team works alternative hours, someone should be available for employee questions during that time. Employees should never feel that they are on their own island because of their work schedule.

If you as their manager aren't available during those times, appoint a project or team lead who can field questions. If you're an employee and this issue has come up, talk with your supervisor about what can help you do your job better. "Greg, even though we're on the East Coast, most of my clients are on the West Coast, and some have emergency issues after our Philadelphia office is closed. Who is my direct contact for after-hours emergency issues? I want to make sure I'm serving the needs of the client and addressing issues as soon as possible. For non-emergency situations, I will let the clients know that we will get back to them by the end of the following business day."

HUMAN CONNECTION

I travel a lot for business and am often in the car or on a plane, but this does not mean that work stops. It just means that I must have systems in place without bogging anyone down. Predictable and consistent questions can usually be sent via email while I opt for a quick huddle or a phone call to explain tasks that require collaboration and more soft skills. If I am not available, I delegate a point person who knows my style of handling these situations. Our team also uses emails and Google Docs to keep track of details and updates.

Because of how many moving pieces my calendar contains, it's best that my Business Development manager, Rebecca, keeps control. She knows who I need to be seeing and who I don't. She also knows how to prioritize opportunities for me and the team. I also have one or two people who ensure that I see and complete timely tasks by the deadline. Do we make mistakes now and then? Sure. But, more so than not, this way of working keeps us moving faster and everyone is happier than the alternative.

Empower those you work with to make the decisions that need to be made so that you don't become the bottleneck to your business. My team is highly effective and productive because the majority of the decisions made can be made by them.

WINNIE SUN, Managing Director and
Founding Partner at SunGroup Wealth Partners

BE HUMAN. ACT HUMAN.

We're all human and can forget to communicate when we're heading on vacation or taking a sick day. (Who feels like emailing from under the covers?) But without taking the extra step to let people know what's going on, you're on the path to losing trust from your team. When you don't make yourself available to answer questions and show and share that you're there to support your employees and coworkers, your relationships suffer. The result is confusion, frustration, and often, high turnover. People don't stay at organizations when they don't feel valued and heard—especially by their direct supervisor and team. A misstep every once in a while is one thing, but a pattern of avoiding clear communication is another. Communicate. Be present. Be accessible.

CHAPTER 14

Going Beyond the Small Talk

IN EVERY JOB I've had, I've always made it a point to get to know my coworkers. I thrive on being in an environment in which I feel connected to the people around me. This may be because I, like most Americans, typically spend more time at work than at home or with family and friends. I'm always sure to secure a work best friend (you know, a WBFF) who I can talk to when my day sucks, and who mutually appreciates my constant need for a sugar fix. Interestingly enough, Gallup data shows that women who strongly agree that they have a best friend at work are more than twice as likely to be engaged in their work than women who say otherwise. In addition, all employees with WBFFs are 27 percent more likely to say that their opinions seem to count at work.[1]

In translation: When you work with people you know, like, and trust, you're more productive and feel more valued in the organization. But finding that person or group of people can be tricky. It's not only about stepping out of your comfort zone but also about creating a space for these professional friendships to form.

Building relationships takes time. Like in the rest of your life, you can't develop a true friend overnight. Even if you're not seeking a full-out friendship, these personal connections build comradery and improve your working relationships. They show that you're interested in what someone else has to say, and you never know what you might have in common.

At one job, after just a few minutes of conversations with my new peers, I found out a coworker and I went to the same high school, another coworker and I had children born a week apart, and a third coworker loved something work-related that I hated and was willing to train me on it (spreadsheets—the part of the job I was dreading most). By opening doors for conversation, you never know what you'll learn. And you can opt to be personal or more reserved based on your own personality.

Personally, I err on the side of full-out friendships. At my last job, my WBFFs were my life. I really don't know what I would have done without them. They would keep me sane when things got crazy, had a constant supply of Swedish Fish at the ready, and put me in my place when I needed to be put there. They were the first to tell me if I acted out of line at a meeting or was getting worked up over something that just wasn't a big deal. Without them, I would have felt lost, unheard, and undervalued in certain situations. We were always there for each other, for the good, the bad, and the reality check.

Although having a WBFF isn't for everyone, most people work best when they have some type of relationship with their coworkers. It's important to feel safe, secure, and valued in the workplace, especially since we know that it's possible we're spending more time in the office than at home. When we find these people, we are even more loyal to the organization as a byproduct of being loyal to the people who work for it.

Get Out of Those Comfort Zones

Building relationships makes a difference whether you're a supervisor, a project lead, or an individual contributor. The problem is . . . it's hard. Sure, it may be simple to strike up some small talk, but chances are, when we do so, we'll just find out when it's supposed to rain this weekend. We don't get to know the people who work with and for us this way. "How about this weather?" will never get us out of the office-speak clouds and into strong, grounded relationships.

At times, you are going to have to put yourself out there and get uncomfortable. Your instinct may be to avoid people when you see them in the hallway, or to come into work 10 minutes earlier to avoid those parking lot hellos. But there are tangible benefits, both professionally and personally, to making the effort and putting yourself out there.

You can start with some baby steps. Try out these conversation starters next time you're walking down the hall or heating up your lunch in the break room:

Future plans. "What are you up to this weekend?" "Do you have anything special planned over the holiday break?"

Celebratory or life event. "I just saw on the calendar that it's your birthday on Saturday. Happy Birthday! What are you planning to do to celebrate?" "Congratulations on your new home. Are you starting to feel settled in?"

Mutual connection. "When I was on Facebook last night, I noticed that we both know Rob Smith. What a small world! How do you know him?" "I've been meaning to tell you that Mary Snyder says hi. She's my new neighbor and mentioned that she graduated high school with you."

Common interest. "Did you see who the Phillies traded last night? How do you think that's going to affect their starting lineup?" "I saw the picture of your new puppy on your desk and she's adorable. We're thinking about getting a German Shepard too. Do you have any suggestions on where to look or what to look for?"

Work question. "I'm working on this spreadsheet for Karla and I can't seem to figure out how to input this formula. I think you use it a lot in your work, right? Can you walk me through it?" "I was so impressed by your presentation yesterday. Are there other resources you would suggest if I wanted to do more research on the topic?"

Compliment. "The macaroni and cheese you made for last week's pot luck was awesome. I've tried to make it before, but it doesn't turn out as tasty. What's your secret?" "You did such an awesome job planning our team retreat. The location, food, and topics were perfect. Where did you find the speaker?"

After you've started the conversation, it's important to ask follow-up questions based on their answers so it doesn't dissolve into meaningless small talk. Show that you're listening and interested in getting to know them better. "That's a great place to have your birthday dinner. I was there a few months ago for a friend's birthday and the cake was amazing. Who are you going with?"

CONVERSATION STARTERS

✔ Ask about future plans.

✔ Congratulate them on an accomplishment.

✔ Ask about a mutual connection.

✔ Share a common interest.

✔ Ask a work question.

✔ Give a sincere compliment.

Keep It Casual

After you start a conversation, it's a good idea to keep it going. Find a good time that works for both of you to continue where you left off. Change the scenery so it's an even playing field and not in a formal office setting. A common option is a coffee shop, but sometimes cafes can be jam packed, or loud, or just not the right fit. Try taking a short walk outside for some fresh air. Or explore a new building—or even just a different floor or area of the building you're in—together. The content of the conversation may be the same, but the location a little different. Getting moving can help get those conversations going.

So, you may walk and chat and strike up a nice exchange. Or you may think, "Whoa, this is a little awkward." And that's OK! If you're struggling to connect, try these questions to take your conversation to the next level.

I'M CURIOUS ABOUT YOUR CAREER	TELL ME ABOUT THE FUN STUFF
■ What was your first job and what did you learn from it?	■ What good books have you read lately? I'm looking for some easy reads for my weekend at the beach.
■ What surprised you the most about this job and our company?	■ Do you listen to podcasts? Are there any that you would recommend for my car ride to work?
■ What was the best career advice you've received and how did that change your perspective?	■ Where is the last place you traveled and who did you go with?
■ What professional organizations have you received value from?	■ Do you have a travel bucket list? What is at the top of the list?
■ What professional development opportunities have enhanced your career?	■ Have you always lived in this area? If so, how has it changed over the years? If not, where did you live before?
■ How do you find balance between your career and personal life?	■ What apps or technology could you not live without and why?
■ What skills are vital to your role and are valued by the organization?	■ What were you like in high school?
	■ Who would play you in a movie?

Keep it light and ask questions that will start to reveal who your coworkers are outside of their job roles. But remember, don't go too deep too fast, and be mindful of things people may not want to talk about with a coworker. "Where was your vacation this summer?" is safe. "Do you want to have children some day?" may not be. We all have different feelings on what is fun to talk about and what is in the "umm, please don't ask me about that" category. So, keep it baseline to start! Travel, hobbies, pop culture. And start to get a sense of how deep to go from there.

HUMAN CONNECTION

To make a personal connection, it's important to be authentic and show sincere interest. As the Director of the Society of Professional Women (SPW), I put together several programs a year with high-profile individuals. When I am going to reach out to an author or speaker, I try to read at least half of their book or watch a few of their videos to be able to point out parts that resonated with me, changed my perspective, or helped me with something. I also share the benefits and rewards of their participation, whether that includes monetary contributions, making further connections, or enhancing their portfolio.

As I start working with them, I like to add personal touches. If they mention a favorite restaurant or favorite color, I incorporate it into my appreciation notes or event details. I try to remember important facts if they open up about their children or personal milestones. If they have a book being released, I set a reminder to reach out. The care you take in the details means a lot. People are much more willing to work with you if you show that you actually care about what they have produced and put some thought into reaching out and keeping the connection.

NICOLE STEPHENSON, Director, Society of Professional Women

Leading (and Connecting) by Example

If you're in a position of leadership, you can use your powers for good. There are many ways to not only provide a space for people to build relationships, but also to model the behavior you're looking for. Relationship-building initiatives create comradery within your organization, help employees feel valued, and take your group to the next level by understanding each other more fully. Try out some of these strategies to get the informal conversations started within your team:

Spend a day on a local cause. Many companies are moving toward paid time off for volunteer work, where you're given the opportunity to take a day and spend it with a cause of your choice. You're paid your daily rate and don't have to use a sick or vacation day. Ask your employees to come up with a few local causes that are meaningful to them and use your volunteer days together. If your organization doesn't have such a program, see if there is an opportunity to set one up. Whether you're doing a clothing drive, planting flowers at a local park, or tutoring kids at a local school, ask others to join you in giving back. Form a team to tackle something close to your heart and use it as an opportunity to connect your team. You can also team up with other local businesses to make an even bigger impact.

HUMAN CONNECTION

My dad and I have owned our custom frame shop for the past 20 years and our involvement in the community goes back over 40 with an active role in the Colonial Neighborhood Council (CNC) food drive. One day when I was bringing in clothes to donate, I noticed how low every shelf was on food. There was only one can of tomato soup and very few other non-perishable items. I decided to put a donation box at my shop and called on a few other small shops to do the same. We all let our existing customers know that food supplies were low and asked if they wanted to donate. There were times when I'd pull up to CNC, start unloading, and families would shop out of the stuff I was bringing in the door. In our first-year volunteering for CNC, we collected almost 7,000 pounds of food over a two-and-a-half-month period. This amount has grown every year since, and this year, we brought in almost 40,000 pounds of food. Although every cause needs all the help it can get, I think the established help comes from people and companies who believe, or who want to be there, which is not part of their job description. People want to connect and help other people. Even the people being helped want to help someone else in another way. If you can, find something you are passionate about and find a way to help someone else.

BRIAN COLL, Owner of Coll's Custom Framing

Unforced happy hours. No employee wants to feel like they're being held hostage at work after hours. No matter how much I love a good glass of wine, it tastes obligatory and uncomfortable if my boss is telling me I have to drink it at 5:00 p.m. on a Friday at work. Instead of extending the work day, think about dismissing an hour early instead. Head to the bar, open a conference room, or congregate around that ping pong table that's collecting dust. Schedule your happy hour during work hours and your employees will feel grateful. If it runs later and people *want* to stay, mission accomplished.

Let the hall conversations happen. In some workplaces, people are discouraged from talking in the hall or judged for not doing their work. I get it, I've been there. It's frustrating when the same people seem to be talking all of the time and it looks like they're not able to figure out where their office is. But you would be surprised at how a quick, "What are you working on?" can turn into, "I can help you with that!" This small talk isn't wasting time. It helps build connections that can enhance teamwork and, ultimately, productivity. It's an outlet and an opportunity to talk informally with colleagues and supervisors. With that said, if you see employees hanging by the water cooler or having conversations in the hall that are starting to interrupt work, bring it up with those specific individuals.

BE HUMAN. ACT HUMAN.

People innately seek human connection, and that doesn't exclude the hours from nine to five. You don't need to be best friends with your coworkers, but you should be . . . well . . . human. Take a minute to thank someone for their work, share some treats, or take a walk. Do some small things together that can take you beyond the small talk and toward real, meaningful connections.

CHAPTER 15

Building a Culture of Trust

"JUST TRUST ME." When was the last time you heard that and honestly felt comfortable? Trust is not something that you can just ask for; it's something that you need to earn. More importantly, it's very easy to lose. People form an ability to trust us based on their interpretations of our actions and not necessarily on our intentions. We need to give our employees, supervisors, and coworkers a reason to trust us by making a positive impact—through our actions and not just our intentions.

A few years ago, I was having severe sinus issues and went to a physician. My experience with the physician involved him shining a light in my nose for about five minutes, followed by a hurried instruction to schedule a surgery for several months out as he practically pushed me out of the door. In that five minutes of face-to-face time with the doctor, I didn't feel we had built a relationship where I wanted to trust him for this procedure. Although he was the expert in the room, and a person of authority, he still needed to earn my trust. I opted to get a second opinion and went with a new physician to perform the surgery because she spent time answering my questions and took an interest in how I was feeling.

This example of doctor-patient trust can be applied to our workplaces. Just because you have a certain title or position doesn't mean that people trust you. Earning it takes time, action, and proven ability.

HUMAN CONNECTION

I'm a big proponent of modeling the behaviors that you want to see in those you lead. My goal is to build teams that are diverse to ensure that we can leverage the different perspectives when working toward an objective. My highest-performing teams have typically included very diverse talent (backgrounds, age, gender, race, culture), and their diversity was not hidden but rather brought forward as an asset.

I recall one team that I inherited after a conflict they ran into with a former manager. This group wasn't cohesively working together due to lack of trust and varying personalities. When I took the role, I decided not to dwell on the issues that led to their former manager leaving the company but instead build a group that could rally around a common purpose. By using our skills and knowledge, we were able to produce high-quality deliverables and work together more closely. It was a difficult challenge, but in the end, the group knew I respected them and they were able to become a cohesive team. It's been over 15 years, and I've had many teams since, but to this day, I am still in contact with several members of that team and consider them to be some of the best talent that I've worked with.

C. COFFEY, VP of a Large Insurance Company

What Is Trust?

Before we jump into how we can earn trust, let's talk about what it is. According to Stephen Covey in his book *The Speed of Trust*, it's made up two components: character and competence. Covey says, "Character includes your integrity, your motive, your intent with people. Competence includes your capabilities, your skills, your results, your track record."[1] Without both of these areas, you'll have a difficult time building and earning trust. People need to know that you're not only genuine and motivated by good, but that you also have the knowledge and skill to be talking about or doing whatever it is that's on your agenda. And just because you've earned trust doesn't mean it's sealed and there to stay. We have to make an active effort to retain the trust of the people who work with and for us. Let's start with how to show you're competent.

HUMAN CONNECTION

I started a new job as the head of an underperforming department that didn't know it was considered dysfunctional by most of the organization. I was hired to "fix" it and quickly discovered I needed to restructure and lay off two of the seven employees. After the two people were let go, I sat down with the remaining staff and explained my reasons for the change and the reality of a new structure, expectations, and responsibilities. Although telling them I had let go of their colleagues was hard, I wanted to be as transparent as possible. I left them as a group to process and told them I'd be in my office and would stay as late as necessary to answer their questions one on one. That afternoon and evening, each person came in to talk to me, and I walked them through my decision and how their job was going to change. Any question was fair game, and I didn't dismiss any concern. I wanted the team to know I would support them with professional development, and that if something wasn't working, we would talk it out and find the right path together.

Although some people were on board quickly, which was an amazing gift, there was one woman who was completely freaked out about the change. She didn't trust me (why should she?), and I could tell a lot was going on under a seemingly calm surface. About a month after the reorganization, during which time I was constantly affirming their work and allowing input into their new roles, she came into my office and just stood there looking at me. She blurted out, "I'm really worried that you are going to hire a new person and then get rid of me like you did the other two people." This was a *huge* deal for her, and frankly, an equally huge relief for me. It showed that I had started to build some level of trust for her to speak so honestly. She ended up being a powerhouse of a colleague who got promoted, and it all started with that slow building of trust.

CELIA C.

Know Your Stuff

Whether you're a supervisor or an employee in a non-leadership role, it's important to know what you're talking about. "Fake it until you make it" won't work here, and it will actually just make the situation worse. If you want to be trusted with information and important assignments, it's essential to stay current with what's going on in your field and to extend your quality of work. Some of the more obvious go-tos are attending conferences or taking a course, but with our busy lives, these are not always an option. A few smaller things that can be folded into our routines include

Setting up Google alerts for your industry on trending topics. You'll get an email every night that pulls together articles for you instead of spending time looking for out-of-date information.

Listening to a podcast on your commute to work. Ask your colleagues and peers for suggestions or check out the top 100 podcasts noted within your listening platform.

Taking an online mini course. Platforms like LinkedIn have short courses taught by experts in the field. They're usually no more than one hour and are made up of many short videos (three to ten minutes) to either watch during your lunch break, in between meetings, or on your train ride home.

If you stay informed in one or more of these ways, when someone asks for your input, you can answer intelligently with relevant information that can be used to make informed decisions. You'll be seen as someone who not only cares about their work but also as a trusted and valuable resource.

Although it's important to stay sharp in your field and contribute your insight to your team, don't be a know-it-all. Be humble in your delivery. Weave your expertise into your work and discussions but don't be the guy that's like, "Well, I just read a 500-page book on how to build more strategic teams. From my expert perspective, we're not utilizing the strengths of our team effectively in your plan. We need to scrap what you've been working on and start again."

Give What You Have

Authentic relationships provide value . . . and value leads to trust. During a meeting or conversation, try to be forthcoming by sharing your expertise, knowledge, and experience. "I was just reviewing those statements and I added a formula in one of the cells. It calculates the percentages automatically so we don't have to go back and forth between spreadsheets. I would be happy to pull up the spreadsheet now and show you if that would be helpful for the other sheets you're working on."

This isn't to show off, but to give someone else information when they either ask directly for it or appear to be struggling and you can help. Don't be pushy or step into situations where you're not invited. For example, if two people are having a private conversation, it's not the time to use your eavesdropping skills to try to be the hero. You don't know the backstory, and butting in can come across as invasion of privacy, no matter how sincere your intentions are. If they move the conversation into the open kitchen area and ask for your input, that's a different story. Once people get to know you and see that you're approachable, and that you want to give advice for the authentic sake of being helpful, trust can begin to build.

Assign (or Ask For!) a Meaningful Project

If you're in a position to do so, give employees the opportunity to make a difference within the organization by assigning them meaningful projects. Not an "order the team lunch" kind of task, but something that lets them show off their skills while pushing the company's mission forward. If you're not a supervisor, ask your boss for a chance to try something new to further show that you can be trusted to complete great things. There are endless possibilities of areas to work on, but here are a few to get you thinking:

- Does the website need to be revamped?

- Are you looking to take the company's social media to the next level?

- Are you launching a product and trying to target a new demographic?

- Is there an innovative way to streamline a process?

- Are you hosting a company-wide diversity training and looking for new speakers and venues?

- Does the organization have affinity or resource groups you could get involved in?

If you're a supervisor providing an opportunity, make sure you're transparent and share

- Professional benefits of taking on the assignment

- Why you chose them

- Deadline and criteria

- Expression of appreciation during the process

- Explicit trust in them to complete this assignment

"Keene, we're looking to enhance our company's online presence and I know you have experience in this area from your side hustle. What you've done is incredible, and I am confident that you can increase engagement on our platforms. We're looking to increase our primary platform followers by 10 percent next month. Social media is starting to play a larger role in our department, and I want to ensure we're working together to build on your skills and set you up for a promotion in the next few months. Is this something you would be interested in having a more detailed conversation about?"

Share with your supervisor your past experience in this area, your plan for this assignment, and why you would be the right one for the job. "I've been working on a social media campaign for my side hustle and have increased engagement by 45 percent in two months. I know social media is something we're really trying to grow, and I know I can do a great job with it. I would start sharing more relevant content, engage with like-minded individuals to increase our reach, and take additional photos for our platforms."

"Yes, and . . ."

When you're in a meeting, show others that you not only heard their contribution, but also that you want to work together and build on their idea by using "yes, and . . . ." This can be a fun way to brainstorm and build trust because now your teammates know you're listening and appreciate their contributions. It also shows that you have experience and insight in this area and are looking to partner up to make their idea happen. Be sure to not fully take over their idea, as it might seem like you're trying to take credit, when in fact, you want to find ways to work together.

> *Ben:* "I think we should have our July retreat at the new outdoor center down the street."
>
> *Christina:* "Yes, and we could bring in Claire to lead us on the ropes course."
>
> *Ben:* "That sounds great. And we can have it catered by the Italian restaurant next door."
>
> *Christina:* "Awesome idea. And I can call Samantha to see what other activities she did when she took her team there a few weeks ago."

You'll see that "yes, and . . ." can come in its literal, verbatim form. Or it takes on some same-meaning synonyms: "Great idea! And . . ." "I love that. And . . ." "That sounds great! And . . ."

Be Present

Just because we're in the same physical space as someone else, doesn't mean we're present. With so many distractions, it seems like it's easy to be texting, answering emails, holding a conversation, and buying a new pair of shoes all at the same time. But people know when you're not 100 percent there. Small things, like making consistent eye contact, make a big impact. Don't think about what you're going to eat for lunch or all of the things on your to-do list; focus on the current conversation. During meetings, make it a point to turn off notifications and leave your phone in your pocket or purse. Once the phone comes out, even if it is face down, it can give the impression that your attention is elsewhere. Unless you're using them to take notes, putting devices out of sight is the way to go.

Being present also means being a part of the conversation and sharing a little about yourself. Even if you know the person you're meeting with already, there's always something new you can share. One-sided conversations don't enhance relationships, and we have to give a little in order for someone to feel comfortable opening up. This isn't about overtaking the conversation and giving your life story or being the "one upper" who always has an experience that's bigger and better; it's just about being relatable and open to sharing your own experiences.

- Were you just as nervous as they are when you started this job?
- Did you try something new and it also didn't work out?
- Did you also just move into town and are looking for the best Chinese food?

When you're having these conversations, listen to the other person and build your questions and stories off of what they're talking about. It's obvious when you're not paying attention when you share an unrelated story or ask questions on information they already covered. Take a deep breath, be yourself, authentically listen, and share your common interests and experiences.

Balance Your Asks with Offers

Be vulnerable, ask for help, and let your employees and supervisors know that you care about their success and the quality of their work. Your being guarded often leads other people to be guarded. When you put yourself out there and ask "check-in" questions, you show that you're human and genuinely invested in what you're working on. Try out these questions during your upcoming conversations:

"How can I support you in your role?" and *"What can I do that would be helpful to you?"* These are great questions to ask your supervisor

and colleagues when you're just starting out in the job, or on a project, or when you notice that someone is struggling and could use your help. It shows that you want to meet them where they are and identify their best interest.

"What might be missing or have been overlooked?" (After you've created the plan, but before you get too far into the project). This gets everyone on the same page and allows for adjustments to ensure you're meeting expectations. It also shows that you want to ensure the success of the project and want to leave no stone unturned.

"Do you have the capacity to do this?" Before assigning additional work, ask your employees if they have room in their schedule for it. Discuss their current workloads and upcoming projects and let them be honest with you about whether or not taking on this additional responsibility is possible. When you ask this question, it's important to listen and respect their response. If they can't take it on, triage with them on alternatives, including alternative people, timelines, or redistribution of work.

"What fires have you had to put out this day/week/month/quarter?" This not only gives you an opportunity to understand some of the challenges and barriers your employees are facing, but it also gives you the chance to do something about it. If you can understand these obstacles, you can provide better support and resources to help them.

"What do you need from me to make this successful?" Ask what you can do to help your employees or teammates complete this work. They might need additional support, people, or material resources. Asking the question shows that you're invested in them and the overall project.

In general, questions that start with who, what, where, when, and why give someone else the opportunity to tell you their story, describe how they're feeling, and ask for the support they need. When we don't ask open-ended questions, we can get yes or no answers that don't help us build trust, a relationship, or a connection.

HUMAN CONNECTION

As a result of a permanent visual impairment in my left eye from an episode of optic neuritis brought on by my multiple sclerosis, I needed to have a very daunting conversation with my supervisor about accommodations. I was mostly blind at the time and was not sure if this would be temporary or if I would eventually be able to see shapes, hard lines, or colors. I was afraid that my team or my boss would lose trust in my skills as a marketing director to design and edit copy. In my conversation, I asserted the fact that they deserve the utmost quality of my work, and in order to provide it, I would need additional monitors to adjust document sizing to leverage a greater attention to detail.

I followed up my request with material that suggested this impairment was actually a superpower. Highlighting this perceived limitation as a strength warranted respect versus pity and admiration versus uncertainty. I was fortunate to eventually regain my vision and was better able to acknowledge and appreciate every detail with more meaning and clarity.

By being open to the conversation and accommodations, my supervisor showed their willingness to be flexible, and I felt appreciated. Everyone thrives in different environments, whether it is the result of a hidden illness or otherwise. Some professionals favor quiet solitude; others prefer loud music and being surrounded by visual and creative inspiration. When employees know they are appreciated, they'll reciprocate by helping break down barriers. My supervisor took the time to acknowledge my needs, provided me with the support I required, and instilled confidence in my team and in me to be successful in our roles.

CHANTEL SOUMIS, Founder and Creative Director, Stardust Creative LLC

Micromanaging: What a Buzzkill

The best way to kill creativity and trust is by *micromanaging*. Avoid sending excessive emails, peering over someone's desk, or showing up every day at 3 p.m. to "just say hi." This can be perceived as a lack of trust for your employee's ability to complete their work. I know it can be hard, because at the end of the day, you're responsible for making sure your team is following through, but you need to give your employees the space they need to show what they're capable of. Don't crowd them. You should, however, be transparent about your needs, deadlines, and the importance of the project. Without transparency, they won't know when things are due, what you're looking for in the task, and how essential it is to the organization. Let your employees know that you're going to give them the space to complete the tasks but that they should reach out to you for questions or if they get stuck. Make yourself available without looking over their shoulder. "I want to give you the flexibility and freedom to complete the project in the way you think is best. But know that I am here to support you if you have any questions or need additional resources along the way. My door is always open."

Although the manager is the one that makes the rules, employees can and should make suggestions to enhance the relationship. People complain about their boss and act like they're powerless to the situation. Which yes, sometimes they are, but often, the employee needs to take some ownership in the relationship as well. They need to take on some tough conversations on their own accord. Writing it off as the boss's job to know what they're thinking or feeling just isn't a fair approach and won't lead to positive change.

When you approach your boss to ask for adjustments, it is key that you do so respectfully, recognizing the hierarchy in your relationship. If your manager is micromanaging, try having a conversation by starting with, "In order for me to be most productive, I need one full uninterrupted business day to work through this project." Or, "Do you mind if I close my door or go into a private work space so I can focus on this project without interruption?" Ultimately, your supervisor wants you to get your work done well. They'll understand they need to give you the space, freedom, and flexibility to be more productive.

Saying Sorry—The Right Way

When you work with different personalities, you may discover that you've lost someone's trust. But that doesn't mean you'll never get their trust back. When you lose someone's trust, it's essential that you get out of your own way, identify why it was lost, be humble, and sincerely apologize. In a study titled *An Exploration of the Structure of Effective Apologies,* Dr. Roy Lewicki found there were six components to an apology, and the more of these components you add, the more likely it is for your apology to be accepted.[2] It's not just saying "I'm sorry" and then moving on. These components are the start to rebuilding trust:

APOLOGY COMPONENT	SAMPLE STATEMENT
Expression of regret	"I am genuinely sorry for making that offensive statement."
Explanation of what went wrong	"I inaccurately used the phrase and did not realize its implications."
Acknowledgment of responsibility	"I accept full responsibility for my actions."
Declaration of repentance	"I not only regret making this statement but have learned that this is not appropriate and will not use it in the future."
Offer of repair	"I registered for a cultural sensitivity training next week because I want to ensure I am more educated on this subject. If you have any additional suggestions, please let me know."
Request for forgiveness	"Please forgive me for my actions."

Based on these six steps, let's go over some key things to avoid when delivering your apology:

Insincere apologies. If you're going to give an insincere apology, you might as well not give one at all. If you're rolling your eyes and using a patronizing tone, the other person can spot it from a mile away. Insincere apologies just make the situation worse. If you need to, take some time to process everything before you take ownership and apologize. It's not about what you intend to say, it's about what you say, and how it makes someone feel. Your tone says it all, here are some examples of what not to do:

- "Yeah, I'm sorry about that." (said with a side eye and a snarky tone)
- "I'm sorrrrry." (said with a long drawn out accusatory sorry)
- "Like I said, I'm sorry." (said in an argumentative and accusatory tone)

Defending your actions. Defending or making excuses doesn't make the other person feel any better. Focus on the other individual, not you. And leave the "coulda," "shoulda," "woulda" out of it. Avoid statements like, "Had you finished the project earlier, I could have answered the email on time. So really, mistakes were made on both sides."

Using indifferent statements. These statements turn the conversation in a different direction, potentially accusing someone else.

- "Brooke, I'm sorry I offended you, but I've been having a really rough week." This brings the conversation back to you and is making an excuse for your actions. Try instead: "Brooke, I apologize for my offensive actions."
- "Cole, I'm sorry **if** I upset you." Not only is this not taking ownership for offensive actions, it also implies that Cole's feelings might not be warranted. Try "Cole, I'm sorry **that** I upset you." Simply changing "if" to "that" provides an absolute statement of apology.
- "Tate, I'm sorry you feel that way." This is not accepting responsibility, while it also implies that Tate's feelings might not be genuine. Try: "Tate, I apologize for my comments that made you feel that way." Similar to the previous suggestions, the adjustment of the language acknowledges the other person's feelings and takes responsibility for your actions.

Although there is no guarantee that using these six components and avoiding these problem areas will rebuild trust, it's a start. When trust is lost, it takes time and continuous effort to make progress in gaining it back. Continuing to have open conversations with your team and individual employees about what they need from you is an ongoing process. All situations and personalities are different, and keep in mind that every solution won't work equally for each person or situation.

HUMAN CONNECTION

I used all my sick and personal days off for child illness and then I had to take another day to be home with my sick son. I went to my supervisor and asked if I could work on a Saturday to make up some of my time. My boss identified a specific project I could work on and went to the director to pitch the idea.

My supervisor then took the time to lay out exactly what I would be doing during that time for the director and why working on the weekend would be beneficial to our company. It meant so much that she went to bat for me. She not only earned my trust, but my sincere respect. As a result, I know that my supervisor and overall company have my best interests in mind, which keeps me motivated to be a top performer.

BRIANA LORA, Biotech

BE HUMAN. ACT HUMAN.

No one is perfect. At some point or another, we'll unintentionally offend a coworker or take an action that could break their trust in us. The difference between the trusted and the untrusted is that trusted people step up, apologize, and take ownership. Trust is hard enough to gain, and once it's lost, it's even harder to earn back. Take the time to build rapport and relationships with others by being present, giving insight, and allowing people the opportunity to shine. Trust is not about showing off what we can do. It's about providing spaces for others to show what they're capable of, while being willing to learn along the way.

CHAPTER 16

Communicating Change
and Embracing It

WE TALKED ABOUT how to open the lines of communication and build relationships with people in your workforce who think, act, and experience life differently than you. But we can't move around a few chairs or add more video conferencing to the mix and expect immediate change and support. Change is hard. It's even harder if people don't feel like they're part of the process.

In this chapter, we're not going to cover the actual change you've chosen to make based on what you've read and how to specifically implement it within your unique and specialized organization. This chapter is all about communicating change. We'll cover

- How to get buy-in from members of your organization (and what buy-in really looks like)

- What to consider if you're an employee affected by change

At the end of the day, it all comes down to including the right people, at the right time, with the necessary information. As a leader (or future leader), one of the key things to acknowledge and ask yourself is this: "We're making a change that affects our company and employees. How do we get everyone on board to make it successful?" Even if you're not in a leadership role, you should be thinking, "What value can I add to successfully help facilitate this change?" Change is good, but selling change can be tough. We need leaders and on-the-ground advocates to make it happen.

Communicating Change as a Leader

To start answering this question as a leader and begin creating a plan of action, you need to ensure that your initiatives consider employees at all levels, from general staff to senior leadership. One of the reasons change may fail is that people are afraid of what they don't know. When you start knocking down physical walls, or even making more minor changes without communicating why, people can question your motives, start making assumptions, and spread rumors. You also cannot assume that everyone will have the same perspective on the change, so you need to be proactive in your communication and get ahead of any chitter chatter. This involves not only being transparent but making an active effort to get people on board before you shake things up and flip the "normal" upside down.

HUMAN CONNECTION

During one of the busiest times of year, one of my colleagues was suddenly let go. Although it may be common in other organizations, this was a rare occurrence for my department. I had worked with this colleague to streamline and improve several processes to better support our office and clients. They provided a high level of support to not only me, but also to our entire department. Their skills in data entry, pulling reports, and institutional knowledge on processes were critical to our daily operations.

At the time they were let go, we were starting an annual large-scale project that required a high level of support. Management did not communicate how we would be redistributing their responsibilities. Fellow members of our team assumed a few of us would absorb my colleague's tasks to complete the project.

Frustrations were high as we had to figure out ways to pull reports or access the information required to complete the project. Suddenly, what took our colleague a few minutes was now taking us hours. It was not until I approached my supervisor that they began to identify how this change would affect our department's workflow. It was still unclear as to how I was to complete my tasks without the necessary support or information.

Many of the frustrations we experienced as a result of our colleague being terminated could have been avoided. If there had been a conversation prior to their departure about their responsibilities to make sure everything was documented, it would have alleviated the confusion over how to proceed with daily functions. We also would have benefited from our leadership being proactive and creating a clearly communicated plan instead of the ad hoc approach that resulted in the team feeling resentful and overwhelmed. Had there been more support and transparent communication from the leadership, we would have been more resilient as an organization and better able to recover from losing a valuable member of our team.

ANONYMOUS

Get to Know Your Employees

This is an ongoing process and shouldn't just happen when change is expected. As a leader, you should always be working to figure out what gets your employees excited, what motivates them, and what tends to make them nervous. We can't assume that our reactions, thoughts, and feelings are the same as theirs. In fact, you *should* assume they'll be different to make sure you get a better understanding of everyone's varied personalities. We all respond to change differently and knowing how to individualize your conversations will not only create a smoother and sustainable change, but more importantly, it will foster authentic relationships.

Reflect back on previous chapters where we discuss employee strengths, generational communication preferences and motivations, accessibility, and ways to earn and retain trust. These strategies and insights will help you engage in better one-on-one conversations with your employees.

Explain Your "Why"

When we're having conversations about things that scare us, our selective hearing mechanisms tend to kick in. So, when you're leading a conversation about change, it's so important to have a clear and consistent message and clearly defined expectations. When having conversations with your team members, make connections on how the new processes, spaces, or whatever else will enhance the success of their individual work, your team's performance, and the overall organization. For example, if you're adding a virtual team meeting once a week, be transparent with your staff and let them know why it's being added, how long you'll meet, and what you will be talking about. Explain the *why*. Specifically, share how adding these meetings will enhance the team and their work. The goal is to empower your employees with a clearly thought-out message that does not leave them making assumptions and questioning your motivations.

When I started in one of my positions in higher education, I was given an office. About four months into the role, a colleague and I received an email that said we would both be moving from our offices into cubicles in the back of the main reception area and that the other three advisors would remain in their office space. The email was very vague and just asked us to pack up our stuff by the end of the week as our new spaces would be ready by then.

We were both confused as to why only the two of us were being asked to move into this space and, of course, we started making assumptions. We began to think we were on our way to being fired and that our supervisor wanted to take a closer look at our performance. Needless to say, we had no idea what was going on and were nervous about this new situation. After we moved to our new spaces, we still hadn't gotten an explanation, and we tried to make the best out of the circumstance. A few months later, we received another email telling us to pack up our stuff and move back into our old offices.

After my then-supervisor moved on to another role, a faculty member explained the situation: they had been thinking about converting our two offices into a new classroom, but the plan did not work out. Although we were relieved to finally hear what had happened, my colleague and I had spent those few months concerned about our performance and too nervous to say anything for fear of being let go. Our supervisor did not communicate why this large change was happening, nor did they ask us for our input to gain a better perspective. Had our supervisor communicated in person as to why we needed to move our spaces, it is likely that my colleague and I would have felt more confident about (or least understood) the need for the change.

Mediums for Intentional Messaging About Change

How we share information about impending changes can be just as important as what we share. If you're making a larger change like moving work spaces, a single email is not going to cut it. This message is something that needs to be addressed in a variety of ways, likely including emails, town halls, and small group meetings. If you're upgrading to more comfortable chairs in the huddle room, a simple email giving employees the heads up is sufficient.

The messaging and choice of medium is your chance to ease concerns, answer questions, and highlight the importance of the change. Identify the level of change you're making and determine the appropriate medium(s) with which to disseminate this message. Review your audience and scale of change to make sure your communication tools best fit the situation to ensure everyone is receiving your message.

HUMAN CONNECTION

One of the hardest parts of being the head of talent management is letting people go. In a former job, I was responsible for implementing a confusing and controversial senior-level process called Top Grading. We had a new CEO and he wanted to clean house because of financial losses and previous poor performance.

All senior-level leaders were to go through an assessment process. A-Players would remain; B-Players could possibly remain; but anyone evaluated as a C-Player (an average performer) would be terminated. Outside consultants created the process and made most of the decisions. I was tasked with the overall communication and implementation details for the company. It was not even a process I endorsed.

I used my network of corporate HR leaders to provide information to the business units. I went on the adage that it's nearly impossible to over-communicate dramatic change, so I used various ways of delivering a much-needed definition throughout the company. This included emails, meetings, one-on-one conversation, and workshops, all to keep employees informed.

Even though this was a hard time for everyone involved, my communication strategies created more transparency for the affected employees. It was important to create clear and consistent messages with such a large change.

BARBARA TAYLOR, Partner of JanBara & Associates

Updates: Less Is Not More

Depending on what you're changing, you might need to make adjustments along the way. It's important to find a consistent method for sharing new information so you don't spring these changes on the stakeholders. When my old office was getting rid of the file room and expanding the kitchen area, our operations team would consistently send us email updates on the progress. These standard emails always had the same branding across the top and used the subject line: "Kitchen Expansion." This subject signaled to readers that this was important information on the renovation while keeping it consistent. It made it easier for us to stay in touch with the progress and for the email to not get lost in the clutter.

Here's another example. Let's say your employees were expecting to have their new workspaces ready in March and that the furniture is on backorder until May. It may sound obvious, but let them know. Don't fear the repercussions of something you can't control, wait until March has come and gone, and then give them the information you've been sitting on (or not sitting on, because you're still without chairs). Go for honesty over unwanted surprises every time.

Being proactive with updates can lead to problem-solving opportunities with your staff and offer a chance to adjust the original plan. You can share updates through an internally shared document, through a weekly email, in individual face-to-face conversations, in town halls, and by discussing them during staff meetings. The success of your change can benefit from consistently updating people with information along the way.

Recruit Change Ambassadors

Although you may need buy-in from the top for change to be successful, you also need support on the ground. Finding the influencers within your organization who can help communicate the change and be its cheerleaders can help take it to the next level. Look for people who others trust. Do others believe in their ideas? Do they produce positive results? These employees can also be a resource to help you identify your communication medium, clarify and promote your messaging, and navigate politics in various departments.

Reflecting back on the strengths chapter (chapter 1), look into the employees that you've identified as influencers. These are the people who can motivate others and get them excited about what's to come. They put others at ease and can help sell your idea.

Talk It Out

Once you get buy-in, it doesn't mean it's guaranteed to stick around. Creating spaces for discussions about the change, asking for feedback, and then acting on the feedback ensures continued support. It's important to follow through and not ignore the dialogue, because in doing so, you'll leave your staff feeling less empowered and more frustrated that you asked and did nothing about it. If someone has spent time to actively participate, reciprocate by acknowledging and acting on it. Or even if you decide not to take action, acknowledge that you heard the suggestion, and explain why you're going to take a different direction.

Equip Them for the Change

Yes, change can be difficult, no matter how big or small it is. When we shake things up, it can be hard to gain support from people who are intimately familiar (and comfortable) with how things are currently working. But why make it more difficult than it needs to be? In order to make change happen, it's essential to remove barriers and provide resources for people to be successful. If you're adding a virtual team meeting and a few members need headsets or a better-functioning camera, make it happen. If you're encouraging more inclusive dialogue among your diverse team members—like diversity discussion or new meeting formats—provide one-on-one coaching and expert trainings to ensure everyone is properly equipped for these new conversations. The more you can ease the stakeholders into this change, the more receptive they'll be to make the adjustment.

Model Change Behavior

Let's not forget that if leaders don't model the change you wish to implement, it will be hard to gain support and get traction. It's like when I eat handfuls of Swedish Fish in front of my kids and tell them they can't have it because it's not healthy. I'm telling them one thing and showing them another behavior. Although employees are not your children, leaders in an organization have a responsibility to demonstrate the behavior they wish to see. Middle managers can monitor daily behaviors, proactively spot any issues or concerns, and promptly address them. Senior leaders can also reinforce, model, and embrace the change while supporting their middle managers in their roles.

EXAMPLES OF CHANGE	COMMUNICATION SUGGESTIONS
New coffee machine in kitchen (small change)	▪ Send an email and place instructions by the coffee maker. ▪ Ensure at least one person understands how to use the new product in case there are questions. ▪ Note this person's contact information on the email and written instructions.
New process for submitting travel reimbursements (medium change)	▪ Send an email and discuss during relevant group meetings prior to the change. ▪ Email and conversations should include information on upcoming trainings on the new platform, contact person for questions, and date of launch. ▪ Once launched, send out an additional email with training information and contact person if they have questions. If possible, include short videos to walk staff through how to use this platform for viewing at their convenience. ▪ Keep track of frequently asked questions and send another email one to two months after the launch detailing the answers to these questions both in text and video walk-throughs.

EXAMPLES OF CHANGE	COMMUNICATION SUGGESTIONS
Moving from closed offices to open floor plan (large change)	■ Consistent and ongoing communication throughout the process is crucial. ■ Recruit change ambassadors who can help spread the message. Equip them with frequently asked questions you expect to answer, specific details about the move, and contact information if they or the people they're speaking to should have questions. ■ Host town halls and small group meetings to explain the change, have employees view the rendering of the new layout, provide contact information to help answer questions, and introduce the change ambassadors. They can also help triage these meetings. ■ Keep all employees updated throughout the process by hosting additional small group meetings and sending email updates with a consistent subject line and branding. Emails can also include links to videos of leadership walking through how the new structure will physically look and how you intend to use the space to help employees visualize the progress and understand how it impacts them. ■ Change ambassadors can host open-door meetings for employees to air their individual concerns. These concerns are then looked into by the appropriate parties and the change ambassadors communicate back the resolution to the employee. ■ Create videos and signs to be placed on new spaces and equipment, and send emails that address best practices for use of new spaces right before the space is complete. ■ Once complete, ensure leadership is modeling best practices of the new space and host a ribbon cutting ceremony. This will not only celebrate the launch of the new space but also is a forum to share contact information for anyone who may have questions; in addition, it shows that your organization is invested in the success of the new layout.

TIPS FOR COMMUNICATING AND IMPLEMENTING CHANGE

✔ Get to know your employees to better cater your communication.

✔ Explain why the change is necessary.

✔ Communicate and then communicate again.

✔ Find and use influencers to help support the change.

✔ Ask questions to understand potential hesitations.

✔ Remove barriers and provide support.

✔ Model the behavior you're trying to implement.

Embracing Change as an Employee

Let's shift gears and talk about employees who are not in a leadership role and are not in a position to make organization-wide decisions.

Even though you're not the one directly responsible for the change, you still have the power to make an impact and advocate for yourself and your team. The key is to do it in a constructive way.

HUMAN CONNECTION

Just because you have always used a blue pen doesn't mean a black pen will be a problem; switching to a black pen might not be necessary, but it's not a problem. Change can provide an opportunity to look hard at procedures and assess them more objectively. Can we do this better? Will this create a better result for our clients? We tend to get very comfortable doing things the way we do them, and it can be easy to forget that sometimes change, even for no apparent reason, can be good. It provides more experience for us to draw on, gives us more options when we're looking for solutions, and enriches us as both people and professionals.

JUDY M.

Ask Open-Ended Questions

Take some time and write down the questions you have right now, and anticipate having, as this change rolls out. These questions might include

- What is my role in this change?

- Who is my contact to ask questions?

- What resources will be available for our team in support of this change?

- What can I do to help ensure the success of this change?

Identify the person to whom it would be best to direct these questions. This might be your supervisor or someone in another department who is more intimately involved in the process. This is not a chance to interrogate, argue, or complain about the impending change; it's an opportunity for an open dialogue to ease your worries.

HUMAN CONNECTION

If you have questions about an organizational change and how it will impact your role, a face-to-face meeting is best. This affords you the opportunity to see someone's body language and get a better understanding through the tone of their voice.

As you're setting up this meeting, send an email as a primer to provide clarity as to what you want to accomplish during the conversation. This also sets up the other person for success. Try using specific language, "I would like to have a better understanding of the staffing changes and how it impacts my role." "I would like to have a list of ideas for how to communicate this message to my team." "I would like to have an agreement on my role during the interim." By using these neutral phrases, you have helped set the tone of the conversation and showed your intention to gain a better understanding of your role to help ensure the success of the change.

ELEANOR LYONS, Partner at Human Edge Resources, LLC

Get on Board . . . Or At Least Try To

During your conversations, it's important to show support and effort toward making this change successful. If this is something you're excited about and believe in, be an influencer to get others on board and ask how you can help. If you're on the fence or don't understand how this will impact you, be proactive and ask questions and gain clarification. You don't want to be the one making assumptions and spreading rumors. Reflect on the tools in this book to gain confidence in asking questions to ease your concerns.

BE HUMAN. ACT HUMAN.

Even the best-intended changes can leave our ever-positive optimists feeling skeptical. But if we keep telling ourselves it's not going to work and make no effort to try, it won't. Try leaving some of that skepticism at the door. We have the power to choose how we'll react to change (and then that change may have the power to make things better). When someone starts complaining about new changes, it's easy to continue the conversation and throw in some negative comments. You need to decide whether to get on board with something new or if you'd rather just walk around being grumpy. Change is not easy. But being someone who can't see beyond their comfort zone won't get you—or your organization—anywhere new, improved, or better.

HUMANIZING OUR
WORKPLACE PLEDGE

To put into action the concepts and strategies you've learned in this book, it's important to make a commitment to yourself, your team, and your organization as a whole. Nothing will change if we're not making an active effort or continuing the conversation.

The following is a sample or starting-off point for your pledge and commitment to bringing a more human element to the workplace. You can create your own personal pledge or work with your team to find verbiage that makes sense for your roles and organization. But just taking the time to solidify your thoughts into strategic actions is the start to creating real human change.

I/We believe humanizing our workplace will enhance collaboration, innovation, and problem solving. It will also increase engagement, empower our employees, and help us stand out as a people-first organization.

I/We commit to creating spaces to share, promote, and include diverse perspectives, backgrounds, experiences, and knowledge where people feel heard and valued.

I/We will inspire others by stepping out of our comfort zone to meet people who think, act, and experience life differently from us.

As advocates for humanizing our workplace I/we will make a conscious effort to support ongoing initiatives, actively listen to others' ideas, accept responsibility for our actions, be open to change, and create spaces for inclusive dialogue.

HUMANIZE OUR WORKPLACE PLEDGE

I/We believe humanizing our workplace will:

I/We commit to:

I/We will inspire others by:

As advocates for humanizing our workplace I/we will:

NOTES

Introduction

1. Annamarie Mann, "Why We Need Best Friends at Work," Gallup: Workplace, January 15, 2018, https://www.gallup.com.

Chapter 1

1. To find out more about these inventories and assessments visit these websites: https://www.gallupstrengthscenter.com, https://www.wiley.com, http://www.viacharacter.org.
2. Jim Asplund, Sangeeta Agrawal, Tim Hodges, and Shane J. Lopez, "The Clifton StrengthFinder 2.0 Technical Report," Gallup, September 22, 2012, https://www.gallup.com, 4, 22.
3. Everything DiSC, "About Everything DiSC: Theory and Research," John Wiley & Sons, Inc. https://www.everythingdisc.com. Accessed on October 29, 2019.
4. "The 24 Character Strengths," VIA Institute on Character, https://www.viacharacter.org. Accessed on October 29, 2019.
5. Asplund et al., "Clifton StrengthsFinder 2.0 Technical Report," 22.

Chapter 2

1. D'Vera Cohn and Paul Taylor. "Baby Boomers Approach 65—Glumly," Pew Research Center's Social and Demographic Trends Project, December 20, 2010, http://www.pewsocialtrends.org.
2. Lindsey Pollak, *The Remix: How to Lead and Succeed in the Multigenerational Workplace* (New York: Harper Business, 2019), 12.
3. Ranstad, "Gen Z and Millennials Collide at Work," July 2016, http://experts.randstadusa.com. Accessed October 22, 2019.
4. Kevin McSpadden, "You Now Have a Shorter Attention Span Than a Goldfish." Time: Health, Neuroscience, May 14, 2015, http://time.com.

Chapter 3

1. Vivian Hunt, Dennis Layton, and Sara Prince, "Why Diversity Matters," McKinsey and Company, January 2015, https://www.mckinsey.com.
2. Office of Multicultural Affairs, "Diversity and Social Justice: A Glossary of Working Definitions," UMass Lowell, https://www.uml.edu. Accessed on October 22, 2019.
3. Office of Multicultural Affairs, "Glossary of Working Definitions."
4. Eli R. Green and Eric N. Peterson, "LGBTQI Terminology," LGBT Resource Center at UC Riverside, 2003–2004, https://lgbtrc.usc.edu. Accessed on October 22, 2019.
5. Office of Multicultural Affairs, "Glossary of Working Definitions."
6. Office of Multicultural Affairs, "Glossary of Working Definitions."
7. United States Census Bureau, "Glossary," US Department of Commerce, https://www.census.gov. Accessed October 22, 2019.
8. Office of Multicultural Affairs, "Glossary of Working Definitions."
9. Harold Andrew Patrick and Vincent Raj Kumar, "Managing Workplace Diversity," *SAGE Open 2,* no. 2 (April 2012)https://doi.org.
10. Avarna Group, "Equity, Inclusion, and Diversity Vocab," North American Association for Environmental Education, https://cdn.naaee.org. Accessed on October 22, 2019.
11. Office of Multicultural Affairs, "Glossary of Working Definitions."
12. Scripps College, "IDEA Initiative at Scripps College: Glossary of Terms," Scripps: The Women's College, Claremont, https://www.scrippscollege.edu. Accessed on October 22, 2019.
13. Scripps College, "Glossary of Terms."
14. Office for Diversity, Equity, and Community Engagement, "Diversity and Inclusion Defined," George Washington University, https://diversity.gwu.edu. Accessed on October 22, 2019.
15. Office of Multicultural Affairs, "Glossary of Working Definitions."
16. Office of Multicultural Affairs, "Glossary of Working Definitions."
17. Office of Multicultural Affairs, "Glossary of Working Definitions."
18. Office of Multicultural Affairs, "Glossary of Working Definitions."
19. Office of Multicultural Affairs, "Glossary of Working Definitions."
20. Office of Multicultural Affairs, "Glossary of Working Definitions."
21. Avarna Group, "Equity, Inclusion, and Diversity Vocab."
22. Office of Multicultural Affairs, "Glossary of Working Definitions."
23. Office of Multicultural Affairs, "Glossary of Working Definitions."
24. Office of Multicultural Affairs, "Glossary of Working Definitions."
25. Office of Multicultural Affairs, "Glossary of Working Definitions."

26. Office of Multicultural Affairs, "Glossary of Working Definitions."
27. Office of Multicultural Affairs, "Glossary of Working Definitions."
28. Office of Multicultural Affairs, "Glossary of Working Definitions."

Chapter 5

1. Association for Psychological Science, "Psychological Science Can Make Your Meetings Better," ScienceDaily, November 9, 2018, www.sciencedaily.com.
2. Bureau of Labor Statistics, "Labor Force Statistics from the Current Population Survey," United States Department of Labor, January 18, 2019, https://www.bls.gov.

Chapter 6

1. Dan Schawbel, "Survey: Remote Workers Are More Disengaged and More Likely to Quit." *Harvard Business Review*, November 15, 2018, https://hbr.org.

Chapter 7

1. Radicati Group, "Email Statistics Report, 2017–2021: Executive Summary," The Radicati Group, Inc., February 2017, http://www.radicati.com.

Chapter 8

1. Marshall McCluhan, "Chapter 1: The Medium Is the Message," from *Understanding Media: The Extensions of Man* (New York: McGraw-Hill, 1964), https://www.bls.gov.

Chapter 9

1. Cecilia RiosVelasco and Nancy Kwallek, "Color and Visual Comfort," Center for Sustainable Development, University of Texas at Austin, School of Architecture, https://soa.utexas.edu.

Chapter 14

1. Annamarie Mann, "Why We Need Best Friends at Work," Gallup: Workplace, January 15, 2018, https://www.gallup.com.

Chapter 15

1. Stephen M. R Covey, *The Speed of Trust*. (Free Press, 2008).
2. Roy J. Lewicki, Beth Polin, and Robert B. Lount, "An Exploration of the Structure of Effective Apologies." *Negotiation and Conflict Management Research* 9, 2 (2016): 177–96. https://doi.org.

INDEX

ABOUT THE AUTHOR

ALISSA CARPENTER is a multigenerational workplace expert and owner of Everything's Not Ok and That's OK, where she provides training, consulting, and speaking services to organizations all over the world. She has a Masters of Education in Social and Comparative Analysis from the University of Pittsburgh, is a Gallup-Certified Strengths Coach, and is accredited in the Strong Interest Inventory and Myers Briggs Type Indicator. Her work helps bridge communication gaps across generations, job functions, and geographies, and she has worked with organizations ranging from nonprofits to multibillion-dollar enterprises. She has delivered a TEDx talk, "How to Humanize Your Workplace One Conversation at a Time, and has been featured in media outlets including *Forbes,* ABC NPR, FOX, and CBS. Alissa lives in Blue Bell, Pennsylvania, with her husband and two children.

Visit Alissa at *www.notokthatsokcoach.com*